Winning in the
Robotic Workplace

Winning in the Robotic Workplace

How to Prosper in the Automation Age

John F. Wasik

PRAEGER®

An Imprint of ABC-CLIO, LLC

Santa Barbara, California • Denver, Colorado

Library of Congress Cataloging-in-Publication Data

Names: Wasik, John F., author.
Title: Winning in the robotic workplace : how to prosper in the automation
    age / John F. Wasik.
Description: [Santa Barbara, California] : Praeger, an imprint of ABC-CLIO,
    LLC, [2019] | Includes bibliographical references and index.
Identifiers: LCCN 2019024588 (print) | LCCN 2019024589 (ebook) |
    ISBN 9781440871665 (print) | ISBN 9781440871672 (ebook)
Subjects: LCSH: Automation—Social aspects. | Robotics—Social aspects. |
    Employees—Effect of automation on. | Labor supply—Effect of automation on.
Classification: LCC HD6331 .W255 2019 (print) | LCC HD6331 (ebook) |
    DDC 650.1—dc23
LC record available at https://lccn.loc.gov/2019024588
LC ebook record available at https://lccn.loc.gov/2019024589

ISBN: 978-1-4408-7166-5 (print)
       978-1-4408-7167-2 (ebook)

23 22 21 20 19   1 2 3 4 5

This book is also available as an eBook.

Praeger
An Imprint of ABC-CLIO, LLC

ABC-CLIO, LLC
147 Castilian Drive
Santa Barbara, California 93117
www.abc-clio.com

This book is printed on acid-free paper ∞

Manufactured in the United States of America

For Daniel James Wasik
Fratres in Aeternum

Contents

Preface

We're all either benefactors or victims of automation in one way or another. If you order something online, the process is highly automated and you can receive what you ordered fairly quickly. When you call your cable, insurance, or credit card company, a robotic voice typically guides you to what you need (if you're lucky). Yet in recent years, the automation age has acquired a new power, presence, and reach that threatens to create mass unemployment—or not. Thousands of stores have closed and hundreds of thousands have lost their jobs.

The debate goes both ways: There will either be an apocalyptic, automated takeover of nearly half the labor force (or more), or so many *new* jobs will be created that it will be something akin to a new employment boon. In this book, I'm exploring both points of view. If both predictions— or just one—are correct, you'll be able to benefit from what I've discovered in more than two years of research.

How I came to this book is a serendipitous journey. Although my interest ranges from the environment and finance to business biography, the history of robotics and automation presented itself first to me through the biography of the great inventor Nikola Tesla. My book *Lightning Strikes: Timeless Lessons in Creativity from the Life and Work of Nikola Tesla* (2016) not only afforded me insights into one of the world's most creative minds, it showed me how automation started with one simple idea. (Tesla, as you'll discover, had a large role in the creation of robotics). More importantly, I managed to do a deep dive into the nature of human creativity, which informs this book throughout (more on Tesla in chapter 1).

What did I learn? Not only was my own creativity challenged in writing the book over a dozen-year span, but I was able to identify what makes us unique as humans. Some of our skills can't be easily duplicated by machines, while automation will probably make difficult, life-shortening labor a thing of the past. We can tap the creative engine within us, although it will take some tweaking, self-reflection, and maintenance.

I'm going to give it to you straight: automation is impacting you and will change the way we work and live in profound ways. Without a doubt, I can say how changes in technology and society have impacted *my* life. A few months before Sept. 11, 2001, my wife and I had built an energy-efficient home in the suburbs of Chicago in a beautiful conservation community. Our oldest daughter was three, with another on the way. But when the dot.com bubble burst, the magazine I was working at (*Consumers Digest*) collapsed with it, leaving me jobless with a mortgage, a mushrooming property tax bill, without health insurance, and two young children—right smack in the middle of a recession.

Little did I know at the time that the Internet, which the publishers of my magazine had staked everything on in building a free website (like most media websites then and now), would become this leviathan sucking advertising dollars out of the print or "legacy" media.

In the ensuing years, once ad-fat newspapers and magazines would succumb to automated advertising generated by the likes of Google and Facebook (and later Amazon). No longer did you need trees, paper plants, printing presses, truck fleets, ad salespeople, or warehouses to generate income. The *online* model was much simpler: once you logged onto a search engine or social media site, the companies running them would use your personal information (such as likes and purchases to display ads), which would, of course, sell you more things 24/7. No salesman would call. No operators were standing by. Advertising, marketing, purchasing, payment, credit approval, and fulfillment were all handled by machines in the blink of an eye.

At first, as the Internet got its legs, I did better than average. I landed a lucrative column with Bloomberg News, itself an overachiever in the automation age. Bloomberg sold real-time market data and analytic tools to money managers and traders all over the world. Since it was an electronic *proprietary* system—renting a terminal cost you up to $24,000 a year—the company didn't have much online competition from free services. The company made Michael Bloomberg, a former bond trader and later mayor of New York City, a multi-billionaire. I profited handsomely, too, until 2008, when the stock, real estate, and credit markets imploded, causing the loss of tens of millions of jobs around the world and a global recession.

Since Bloomberg had lost thousands of customers in a crash that cratered several Wall Street trading firms (Bear Stearns, Lehman Brothers), it had to retrench, so it dropped my column in the fall of 2009. That was a horrible year for me and my family as the job loss was punctuated by my wife's cancer diagnosis, surgery, chemotherapy, and radiation treatment. With two children and practically no income, I had to rebuild my journalism career just as the mainstream media business was shrinking due to the Internet advertising cyclone. Luckily, I managed to land columns with Reuters—Bloomberg's principal rival—and several other online publishing platforms, although none of them lasted.

Longtime publishing giants, too, became victims to the proliferation of automated and aggregated free news. Why pay for a newspaper or wire service if you could get news from everywhere for free generated by software that would curate your every interest from cat videos to foreign affairs white papers? The entire Time Inc. empire is mostly dismembered. Local newspapers all across the United States. are struggling to keep their doors open while firing tens of thousands of journalists (more on that later). The largest and most storied publications such as *The New York Times* and *The Wall Street Journal* (both of which I've written for), are charging for digital subscriptions and running in place to offset the loss of print advertising dollars, which seemingly shrink every quarter. They, too, have fired legions of fine journalists.

In recent years, as I slowly and painfully shifted away from mainstream media—being repeatedly burned by diminishing editorial budgets—I had to do some rigorous self-examination: What did I *need* to know in an age in which information was commodified and given away every second of the day? Which firms were going to survive? What skills did *I* need to enhance or develop? How could I make it to retirement age, pay my bills, and survive doing what I truly loved, which was writing, reporting, and speaking? The answers to those questions, I humbly submit, are mostly in this book, which I hope will serve anyone struggling against the tide of the machine maelstrom that's consuming nearly every industry.

Think of this book as a lifeboat that's buoyed by human creativity and many other skills—*your* skills. This multifaceted part of human nature may not save everyone faced with the annihilation of jobs in the automation age, but it will serve as a tool for future growth—and something everyone can employ.

Acknowledgments

Many thanks to my former editors, Zach Gajewski and Hillary Claggett, and my current editor, Kevin Downing.

Special thanks to Prof. Rob Twardock at the College of Lake County, the University of Chicago's Polsky Center, Fred Beuttler at the Graham School, Prof. Robert Shiller, and the Illinois Holocaust Museum (Marcy Larson).

Such a project wouldn't have been possible without the countless professionals working in colleges, public libraries, business incubators/accelerators, and schools throughout the country. You are the foundation of knowledge and the spirit of democracy.

My teachers have been a profound influence on my life and career as well. Without them, I don't know how I would've challenged the world. Special thanks to Mary Freund, Wayne Erck, and Erma Amstadter.

Most importantly, thanks to my daughters Sarah and Julia and my wife Kathleen, whose love, support, and inspiration are boundless. And to my late baby brother, Daniel James, to whom this book is dedicated.

Introduction

Robots and AI tools are invading the workforce en masse. Reports from the White House, McKinsey, and Oxford University confirm one of the most disturbing trends since the advent of the Industrial Revolution: much of the workforce across the world can and *will* be automated. This is an overview of what to expect based on different points of view.

What makes us *human* will allow us to survive and prosper, although few know exactly what skills and qualities are most important. This book examines that question in great depth. The answers will surprise many. We've been alerted to the problem in many ways in recent years. President Obama warned us on the way out of the White House:

"The next wave of economic dislocations won't come from overseas," the president's team said at the end of his second term in 2016. "It will come from the relentless pace of automation that makes a lot of good, middle-class jobs obsolete."[1] It's already happened and will be the biggest societal sea change of our time.

What's changing? Let's look inside the White House study, which came out in the last month of the Obama administration and was mostly ignored at the time.

- Every three months, about 6 percent of jobs in the economy are destroyed by shrinking or closing businesses, while a slightly larger percentage of jobs are added—resulting in rising employment and a roughly constant unemployment rate.
- The economy has repeatedly proven itself capable of handling this scale of change, although it would depend on how rapidly the changes happen and how concentrated the losses are in specific occupations that are hard to shift from.

- Research consistently finds that the jobs that are threatened by automation are highly concentrated among lower-paid, lower-skilled, and less-educated workers. This means that automation will continue to put downward pressure on demand for this group, putting downward pressure on wages and upward pressure on inequality.

- In the longer run, there may be different or larger effects. One possibility is superstar-biased technological change, where the benefits of technology accrue to an even smaller portion of society than just highly skilled workers. Instead of broadly shared prosperity for workers and consumers, this might push toward reduced competition and increased wealth inequality.[2]

Although this report has since been augmented by other research, which we'll explore, it lays the groundwork for a bleak employment picture. Only a few workers with the appropriate skills for the automation revolution will prosper, while millions—possibly up to half of the workforce—will be left behind.

There's also one major shortcoming in the White House study: it primarily focuses on artificial intelligence. Yet there are myriad other technologies that are reducing the need for human labor that are not discussed in the report. Robotics, for example, is eliminating certain kinds of jobs in everything from auto manufacturing to warehousing. That's been an ongoing trend in nearly every heavy industry, which we will examine in the first two chapters.

THE MCKINSEY STUDY: WHO LOSES THEIR JOBS

A year after the White House study appeared, the McKinsey Global Institute published *Harnessing Automation for a Future That Works*, which addressed many of the labor-elimination issues raised in the Obama administration report.[3]

While the McKinsey team estimates that "fewer than 5% of occupants are candidates for full automation," large swaths of the future workforce can be automated piecemeal.[4]

- We estimate that about *half* of all the activities people are paid to do in the world's workforce could potentially be automated by adapting currently demonstrated technologies. That amounts to almost $15 trillion in wages.

- The activities most susceptible to automation are physical ones in highly structured and predictable environments, as well as data collection and processing. In the United States, these activities make up 51 percent of activities in the economy, accounting for almost $2.7 trillion in wages. They are most prevalent in manufacturing, accommodation and food service, and retail trade.

- It's not just low-skill, low-wage work that could be automated; middle-skill and high-paying, high-skill occupations, too, have a degree of automation potential.

- Our scenarios suggest that half of today's work activities could be automated by 2055, but this could happen up to 20 years earlier or later depending on various factors, in addition to other economic conditions.

As with nearly every social-technical change from printing presses to AI, nothing happens all at once. The tsunami that both reports suggest will happen incrementally as technologies mature and are adapted in the workplace.

It's also wise to take into account that humans will not only lose work to machines, they will also work *alongside* and with them, integrating their skills with those of machine learning. The McKinsey authors observe this gradual transformation: "Even when the technical potential exists, we estimate it will take years for automation's effect on current work activities to play out fully. The pace of automation, and thus its impact on workers, will vary across different activities, occupations, and wage and skill levels."[5]

I disagree with their conclusion: The impact of automation is happening *now* and playing out every day. And we're not prepared for it.

THE OXFORD STUDY: AN ARGUMENT FOR OPTIMISM

The White House and McKinsey reports were built on the groundbreaking insights by two researchers at Oxford University, who asked many of the same questions about automation and the future of work.[6] The Oxford authors used a 1930 essay by the great economist John Maynard Keynes as a launching point. Keynes boldly predicted that automation would eliminate a significant amount of human labor in the future at a time when there wasn't enough paid work to go around during the Great Depression. Although Keynes was wrong about *when* this would happen, he wasn't far off the mark on *why* it would happen. Even during the height of an economic catastrophe that would trigger another world war, Keynes could see that technology would make many forms of human labor obsolete. (More on Keynes in the next chapter.)

As researchers who informed the White House and McKinsey researchers, the Oxford group suggested a gradual shift toward automation in a select number of industries:

- Our model predicts that most workers in transportation and logistics occupations, together with the bulk of office and administrative support workers, and labor in production occupations, are at risk.
- Our findings thus imply that as technology races ahead, low-skill workers will reallocate to tasks that are non-susceptible to computerization—i.e., tasks requiring creative and social intelligence.
- As technology races ahead, low-skill workers will reallocate to tasks that are non-susceptible to computerization—i.e., tasks requiring creative and social intelligence.[7]

While I dispute the Oxford authors' assertion that "low-skill workers will reallocate" to better, nonautomated jobs—this will require a deliberate and massive cooperative effort by government, industry, and nonprofits—I share their optimism for the ability to recognize *which* jobs are most imperiled. There's much we can do to prepare for these changes.

TWO EXPERTS PROVIDE PERSPECTIVE

There's much more to the automation job-loss debate that is getting far less attention than the sphere occupied by the Oxford, McKinsey, and White House reports. In the growing field of automation research, two of the most prominent scholars are Daron Acemoglu of MIT and Pascual Restrepo of Boston University. Not only have they written extensively on the subject, their voices are well respected and often quoted (I refer to them extensively in coming chapters).

While Acemoglu and Restrepo agree that jobs will be lost to automation, the scholars also say that the job rout *isn't* inevitable. Many employers may choose to retain human labor, although the trend is clearly going in the opposite direction. In three papers, they are quick to show how automation has replaced hundreds of thousands of jobs in recent decades.

But have the old, eliminated jobs been equally replaced by new, higher-paying positions, as many critics of the automation labor rout contend? They note: "automation by itself *always* (italics mine) reduces the labor share in industry value added and tends to reduce the overall labor share in the economy (meaning that it leads to slower wage growth than productivity growth)."[8]

"It's about choices," Acemoglu told Axios. "So far, we've used our know-how singularly automating at the expense of labor. If we keep on doing that, we will keep on destroying more jobs without job gains. It's completely our decision."[9]

THE BOTTOM LINE FOR THE FUTURE

How do we prepare billions of people for the mega-automation of entire industries? This book digs into these global trends and breaks them down into a challenging narrative: How did we get here? Who are the winners and losers? How do we reclaim the dignity—and prosperity—of work?

The reality of today's automated economy is snuffing human jobs by the day. Call center jobs are replaced by "smart" voice-mail systems. Entire steel mills are mostly run by computers. Elon Musk's new "gigafactory" is making millions of batteries with robots. Everything from legal work to more than 1 billion press releases is automated. The grim reality is that not only are manufacturing and heavy industry scaling up for even more automation—those coal mining jobs are *not* coming back—but millions of *white-collar* jobs will be eliminated as well.

BOOK STRUCTURE

This book creates a framework for how to view the old and new skills needed to survive in the age of automation. After a brief history of automation, I'll show you how particular industries have been impacted and how the combination of robotics, artificial intelligence, and other machine systems are changing nearly every industry.

I'll identify specific occupations and skills that will be in demand—or can be integrated in new ways—to allow you to prosper in the evolving workplace. Innovation, discovery, and collaboration will be essential bricks in this building (or rebuilding) of your skill set. I'll also highlight some of the essential cognitive, social, and emotional skills you'll need to prosper and where to build those skills.

What makes this book unique is that it won't belabor the fact that a large portion of the workforce will be automated. Instead, it will focus on the specific "Quad I" skill set that I believe will better enable workers and professionals to prosper in the age of automation.

The key is understanding that human skill sets and the most powerful tools we have: *creativity, conceptualization, and collaboration.* These three instruments of human intellect and personality will help us survive the inevitable automation onslaught. In rich narrative detail, this book will tell the story of the winners and losers while charting a way forward.

I'll also show the power of becoming a Quad I who can harness innovation, integration, insight, and improvisation to thrive in an automated workplace.

WHAT IS THIS BOOK FOR?

This book will briefly examine the history of robotics and automation and look at what massive automation means for the present and future of labor. The narrative, though, isn't of darkness and despair. It's about people and how they learn new things and become more human. From steelworkers to sophisticated designers, I'll tell their stories and what they are doing now.

Which jobs have been and will continue to be eliminated by automation? Why is our educational system woefully underprepared for this unstoppable change? What kinds of skills will enable us to navigate this transition?

Robots and AI may be taking over millions of jobs, but there's a lot of things they can't do. This book offers key insights into what skills will be invaluable for those who are prepared.

But this will be more than just a look at the history, promise, and perils of robotics: it will be a journey that will challenge everything we know about work, prosperity, and what it means to be human. The book spans my initial writing on labor issues beginning some 40 years ago and takes the reader well into the future. I'll take the reader from the steel mills of South Chicago to the cybernetic world of Wall Street. You'll meet the leaders and losers of this new revolution.

The subject is a natural extension of subjects I explored in *Lightning Strikes: Timeless Lessons in Creativity from the Life and Work of Nikola Tesla* (2016). I've also explored the narrative approach combining storytelling, history, technology, finance, and sociology in my books *The Cul-de-Sac Syndrome* (about the 2008 housing crisis) and my award-winning

The Merchant of Power: Samuel Insull, Thomas Edison, and the Creation of the Modern Metropolis (2005).

WHO IS THIS BOOK FOR?

Any reader concerned about the future of work, technology, and education will find some useful information in these pages. Although it will mostly appeal to younger workers, it will engage engineers, policy makers, economists, educators, and anyone interested in technology and the evolving nature of work. Anyone who wants to employ their creativity will also benefit.

The book will also appeal to those interested in robotics, the Internet, technophiles, Silicon Valley, and venture capitalists. There will be special interest for younger "makers," those experimenting with coding, robotics, and new technology.

FINAL NOTES

This book will address the skills that will allow us to successfully merge and prosper in the age of automation. I will detail what you need to know, how to better educate yourself and prepare for the ultimate nexus between machine and human intelligence.

You'll meet the leading thought leaders in academia, government, and corporate realms who are effectively navigating change. Ultimately, you'll come away with a tool kit for best addressing automation and understanding how these changes will impact nearly everything we do.

ONE

Tesla and the Teleautomaton: A Brief History of Automation

This chapter begins with Nikola Tesla inventing and demonstrating the first robotic device, a radio-controlled boat in Madison Square Garden in 1898. How Tesla came to this idea will begin the narrative on our need and desire to automate everything from factory work to warfare. I'll profile early forms of automation and how robots came into the workforce in many forms.

When Nikola Tesla invented and demonstrated a wireless, robotic boat at the old Madison Square Garden in 1898, it begat entire industries in robotic manufacturing and, eventually, driverless vehicles.

The tub-shaped, radio-controlled craft showed the world how devices could be controlled remotely and heralded the birth of what Tesla called "teleautomatons," or robots, a word that didn't exist yet. Tesla, the father of alternating current, radio, and wireless transmission of electricity, had done something remarkable. While his invention wasn't even called a "robot," it demonstrated how a remotely controlled machine could work. It would be decades before the potential of his machine could be recognized, of course, but it would eventually change the future of human labor.[10]

A year after his New York debut, Tesla brought his robotic boat to Chicago, where he demonstrated his device before hundreds in the legendary Auditorium Theatre, renowned for its perfect acoustics. This time, though, he was talking about a remote-control torpedo. It took him a year to weaponize the technology that would change the world, although he abandoned his weapon-oriented experiments to build a "World System" that could broadcast electricity. (Note: Military drones emerged from Tesla's experiment, although nearly a century later. Now remote-controlled weapons are widely used in modern warfare. While the exact tally has not been published, thousands have been killed and injured by drone strikes. There are currently more than 7,000 U.S.-operated military drones with more than 200 of them believed to be armed, according to New America Foundation's International Security website.)[11]

What was important about Tesla's machine? It combined a means of *remotely* controlling a device that could do specific tasks. Utopians and others, however, thought that Tesla's concept of remotely applied labor would reduce the number of tedious and dangerous tasks in the workplace— everything from assembly lines to coal mining. The device even employed what Tesla called a "logic gate," which was a forerunner to a semiconductor. Despite his groundbreaking progress in thrusting the automation age forward, Tesla's thoughts, inspired by the philosopher René Descartes's views that *people* were essentially mechanistic—controlled by outside energy—veered far into the future.

> It would be possible to construct a machine that would have the arms and legs, and which would walk in an upright position, but this would additionally complicate the task and make it more complex.[12]

When writing about teleautomatons in the late nineteenth and early twentieth century, Tesla's prescience foreshadowed artificial intelligence and an integration of learning and machine work. He was envisioning creating "a machine which would work as if it were part of a human being, not only a mechanical assembly . . . but a machine embodying a higher principle which would allow performing their duties as if it possessed intelligence, experience, logic, reasoning, soul!"[13]

Sadly, Tesla never profited from his robotics insights and automation dreams. He staked his fortune on broadcast (wireless) electricity, but lost everything when financiers pulled their support from his grand experiment on Long Island around the time of World War I. Nevertheless, the Second Industrial Revolution, ushered into being by the mass introduction of cheap, widely available alternating current into factories, offices, and homes, made possible exponential improvements in productivity. If you work later by artificial light, you could make more things in a longer workday. You could keep food cold, heat and cool every interior space, and even vacuum your carpets (no more rug beaters!). Electric motors and widespread alternating current delivered to most urban locales meant less labor and more leisure time, something only the rich could ponder before the electrical age.

BACK TO KEYNES'S PREDICTION

As a younger contemporary of Tesla, John Maynard Keynes was another heralded genius whose predictions and insights were often ignored. As a young member of the British diplomatic team at the Versailles Treaty talks after World War I, Keynes made a frightening prediction that the draconian economic reparations imposed on Germany by the allies would lead to another war. Keynes also had a pretty amazing crystal ball, which he would use to examine other societal trends.

In his famous 1930 essay "Economic Possibilities for Our Grandchildren," Keynes peered beyond the Great Depression—which he helped major Western governments tackle—into the future of work. Even as the world was lurching toward war, economic despair—"a bad attack of economic pessimism"—and catastrophic destruction, Keynes was foreseeing a future that would involve dramatically less human labor—and significant free time:

> In quite a few years—in our own lifetimes I mean—we may be able to perform all of the operations of agriculture, mining and manufacture with a quarter of the human effort to which we have been accustomed. . . . We are being afflicted with a new disease . . . namely technological unemployment. . . . All this means is that in the long run *that mankind is solving the economic problem.*[14]

Keynes was essentially optimistic in this landmark essay. While acknowledging that jobs would be lost to new, labor-saving technologies, he saw the virtues of having less work to enjoy more fulfilling lives filled with purpose and meaningful pursuits. That was the bright side of "technological employment." It lightened the burden of the "economic problem," that is, having to work long hours to pay bills. Unfortunately, while Keynes's prediction on job loss and productivity gains came to pass, the lighter side of his vision was a Faustian bargain, as we'll see in later chapters.[15]

Of course, both Tesla and Keynes stood on the shoulders of hundreds of other innovators throughout history. Here's a summary of that timeline:

A BRIEF HISTORY OF AUTOMATION

- Ancient "automata" are recorded around 400 BCE in ancient Greece and China. They are crude machines that only perform one task.

- The first "programmable" automaton was invented by Heron of Alexandria in the first century BCE. Automatons are also noted in India, Rome, the Byzantine Empire, and the Islamic world. They are powered by water, gravity, and pneumatics, eventually leading to the first clocks.

- Devices emerge throughout Europe during the Middle Ages, mostly in the form of crude, moving objects and even more sophisticated clocks. By the end of the eighteenth century, a clock becomes so accurate that it can allow mariners to calculate longitude.

- A talking brass head, reportedly created in the twelfth century by Albertus Magnus, is said to be powered by steam. The young philosopher Thomas Aquinas, the legend goes, is so shocked he smashed the device to pieces.*

- The industrial age, beginning in the late eighteenth century, uses devices ranging from "programmable" looms to independent steam locomotives and the railroad era. The widespread mining of coal and application of steam energy revolutionizes labor. The first automatic pumps are used to drain coal mines.

- The late nineteenth century witnesses an explosion of new machines from higher-powered dynamos (electrical generators) to large-scale, high-voltage electrical systems. The second industrial age, still largely powered by coal and steam, dramatically reduces physical labor with the advent of Tesla's AC motors, hydraulics, and later electronics.

- The term "robot" is first used by Czech playwright Karel Čapek in his 1921 play *Rossum's Universal Robots*. Čapek's robots are "organic artificial humans."

- A new machine invented by French tennis star René Lacoste automates the delivery of tennis balls in 1927. Fritz Lang's silent movie *Metropolis* introduces a golden, humanoid robot.

- In 1928, the U.S. military introduces a new "tracking anti-aircraft gun," which they call a "robot." Makato Nishimura builds a humanoid robot the same year that mimics facial expressions.

- Westinghouse designs and exhibits a walking robot called "Elecktro" at the New York World's Fair (1939–40)

* Daniel Wilson, "Fear of a Robot Planet," Politico, Aug. 4, 2017.

(continued)

- Programming and automation receive a major boost from defense funding during and after World War II, ranging from Alan Turing's programmable code-deciphering computer to the first basic digital "mainframes" used in military and industrial applications.

- The Cold War and Space Race throw computing and automation into overdrive as the United States and the Soviet Union race to put a man on the moon (1969). GM and other automakers begin to use robots in their plants.

- The digital age moves into full swing in the decades during and after the Cold War, with ever-larger computer systems handling massive amounts of data processing. Companies like BM become global giants and develop powerful artificial intelligence platforms like "Deep Blue" and later "Watson" that can beat humans at chess and the game show *Jeopardy.*

- The Internet age blossoms with the widespread use of what was originated by the Pentagon (the ARPAnet). Now, anyone with a computer and phone line could access nearly any database and untold processing power from home computers. Companies like Apple, Amazon, Facebook, and Google emerge to harness this new information revolution to automate everything from music sharing to warehouse logistics.

The curve of progress, you may note, turns steeply upward the more technology comes into widespread acceptance. Having a wide group of global companies, governments, and entrepreneurs working on automating every industry tends to speed up the development of new applications and machines.

Then there's the economic incentive: companies faced with rising labor costs will turn to machines. Robots don't need pensions, health care, or paid vacations (except for maintenance). As wages rise around the world, the profit motive focuses ever more on putting robots in the workplace instead of people—and that trend is accelerating.

"It took 50 years for the world to install the first million industrial robots," note Bloomberg writers Chris Bryant and Elaine He (writing in 2017). "The next million will take only eight."[16]

To date, most automation has occurred in heavy industry. Robots have taken over routine assembly tasks in nearly every manufacturing setting. They put parts on vehicles and run merchandise through warehouses. They even keep workers away from dangerous situations such as pouring hot steel.

It's hard to argue that this benefit of automation has saved or prolonged lives and removed workers from tasks that were life-numbing.

Yet automation always comes at a cost. Daron Acemoglu and Pascual Restrepo estimate that up to 670,000 American jobs were replaced by robots between 1990 and 2007.[17] Does the United States have a comprehensive program to retrain workers who lost jobs to automation? Job-retraining efforts have been insignificant. Other than the White House, Oxford, and McKinsey reports (cited in the introduction), there has been no concerted global call outside of academia to directly address meaningful employment policy to offset massive job dislocation.

Still, the question remains: how to adapt to these changes in a way that gives workers of today and tomorrow more flexibility and the most-usable skill sets? First, it's necessary to accept the reality that jobs will be cut in large numbers:

"One thing is clear," notes technology writer David Pogue. "Robots are definitely going to take over millions of our jobs. About 5 million retail jobs, 3 million truck driving jobs and 500,000 taxi and ride-sharing jobs could, in time, take their place alongside the millions of factory jobs that robots have already displaced."[18]

While it's true that the word "disruption" is overused when referring to technology, it's not being overly pessimistic to suggest that whole industries are being transformed. Self-driving vehicles pose a threat to taxi and truck drivers. Why pay for a human driver when you can run a machine that runs 24/7 by itself? Such vehicles will likely run on electricity and be able to recharge themselves—and they won't fall asleep at the wheel and will largely avoid accidents.

Again, the picture is not black and white. While some middle-level jobs may be automated, some low-skilled jobs will remain—and even be in more demand. A nuanced view is needed to understand how automation will impact the labor market today and in the future.

Michael Gibbs, a business professor at the University of Chicago, notes that certain worker skill sets will offer better opportunities than others. And there are some surprises, he notes:

The labor market has become polarized: while middle-skill jobs become increasingly automated, high-skill jobs that require a combination of cognitive skills, creative acumen and leadership expertise have not been affected. Similarly, low-skill jobs that require customer service or rely on teamwork have not been as drastically changed by automated systems. Therefore, it is the middle-skill, routine occupations that have been decimated by the technological revolution.[19]

The dire scenario of massive unemployment may not occur the way experts say it will—we are going through a chimeric transition where we learn how to *merge* human skills with those of machines. *If so, a new postindustrial renaissance is underway.*

Still, the innovations needed to improve overall job growth, address global warming, and create shared prosperity won't come without a disruptive shift in public education, employment training, and political institutions.

FINAL NOTE: WHY ROBOTS AND AUTOMATION ARE A THREAT TO EMPLOYMENT

Throughout the genesis of the Second Industrial Revolution, the specter of robots and automation cast a dark cloud over humanity. We're now in a Third Industrial Revolution where smart machines will take over physical and many intellectual tasks. It may be a damaging deluge or gentle showers that bring May flowers. It depends where you're standing in the thinking machine age. The next chapter will explore which industries and jobs are most imperiled.

Like his contemporary Tesla, Keynes was a fervent believer in the power of technology to liberate humanity from tedium and drudgery: we'd simply have more time to enjoy the arts and leisure because machines would liberate us from mundane tasks. While technology hasn't quite accomplished that goal, the obverse of the automation scenario is that we can be liberated to do things we're really good at *and* still prosper.

The next chapter will focus on specific trends in workforce automation and recent history. Some occupations are getting hit harder than others. Prospering in the automation age will largely depend on how you respond to large-scale changes. But first, let's take another look at what's happened to specific professions in recent years.

TWO

Automation Acceleration: Why Robots Are Coming for Your Job

As the United States, Japan, and Europe built up their industrial base before and after World War II, automation was always eyed as a way of making factories more efficient with less workers. In the postwar era, this trend got incremental traction, although it really took off in recent years. This chapter will summarize how automation came to heavy industries. I'll also discuss how artificial intelligence and machine learning are accelerating the automation trend in today's factories, offices, workplaces, and warehouses.

Derrick Smith worked at Wisconsin Steel in Chicago as a laborer in the late 1970s. While it didn't require much skill and was often dangerous, it was a good job for the time. He had union benefits such as a pension, paid vacation, and health care. He was moving up the ladder into the middle class (I have changed his name to protect his identity and dignity).

Seemingly without warning, the mill closed March 28, 1980, leaving more than 3,400 workers out on the street. I was covering the mill's closure for the local paper on the southeast side of Chicago, *The Daily Calumet.* Like most steel mills in the United States at the time, Wisconsin Steel hadn't invested enough capital to keep up with current technology, which favored smaller, more automated "minimills" that were operating in the South and overseas. Years before, Wisconsin Steel was spun off to a holding company that didn't have the money to invest in the plant. A "captive" mill that was previously owned and operated by International Harvester to make agricultural implement parts, the tiny mill didn't stand a chance when the impact of a massive Harvester strike and global recession hit around 1980.

The Wisconsin Steel debacle, however, wasn't an outlier and would be only one of many dramatic shifts in the industry.[20]

Mills throughout the Calumet region of southeast Chicago and northwest Indiana (and throughout the United States) would either shut down or be sold at virtual fire sales to overseas holding companies, which would immediately downsize union labor forces and mostly automate some of the oldest and best-known mills in North America. One by one, the mill shutdowns continued: U.S. Steel's South Works, Jones & Laughlin, Republic Steel, Youngstown Sheet and Tube, Inland Steel. The original operating companies would either disappear or be acquired by other companies. Mighty U.S. Steel, founded by Andrew Carnegie and J. P. Morgan around the turn of the twentieth century, would eventually shutter all but one of its mills in the Chicago area. The footprint of U.S. Steel's South Works is still an empty lot the size of the entire Chicago Loop as I write this.

A SNAPSHOT: AUTOMATION IN THE STEEL INDUSTRY

If there was ever a prime candidate for automation, steelmaking was on the top of the list 40 years ago. It wasn't unusual for the largest steel mills to employ at least 20,000 workers. The oldest technology—open-hearth furnaces—were like giant fireplaces in which steel was formed by thousands of men shuffling metal throughout a dangerous environment. If molten metal came into contact with water, it resulted in a deadly, violent explosion. Most of the labor involved in producing it was semi- or unskilled, which offered employment to hundreds of thousands of laborers from the Deep South to Eastern Europe.

The southern end of Lake Michigan was crowded with steel mills from Waukegan to Gary. Companies like Bethlehem, Inland, Youngstown Sheet and Tube, and the goliath U.S. Steel each had mills, which made everything from sheets for autos and appliances to specialty products like alloy and stainless steel. The mills anchored the Calumet Region because of its proximity to iron ore mines in Northern Michigan and Minnesota, coal from the south, and limestone from throughout the Midwest, which is the bedrock of Illinois and Indiana. Iron ore would be mixed with refined coal (coke) and limestone in multistory blast furnaces, then rolled or formed into sheets, bars, and rods. It was this Promethean mastery over nature that made possible the mass production of the modern age—everything from transcontinental rail-roads to skyscrapers to a car in every driveway. Being on an inland water-way also was essential; the mills could barge iron ore from the upper Great Lakes to the lower lakes cheaply in massive ore boats the size of city blocks. Barge transportation then (and now) was one of the cheapest forms of transportation. Other mills located near rivers in Pennsylvania and Ohio.

Yet traditional steelmaking was labor and energy intensive, and the old-est operations weren't generally supplied with the capital to keep up with advances such as basic oxygen and electric-arc furnaces that could be auto-mated using hundreds of fewer workers. Overseas operations and mostly nonunion minimills in Southern states effectively competed with the older, mammoth mills with steel that could be produced at a lower cost per ton.

The largest mill in the region—U.S. Steel's Gary Works—provides a typical example. The former open-hearth operation went through a radical downsizing as technology changed. In 1978, the northwest Indiana mill employed more than 21,000 workers. Now it's less than 7,000. The biggest job losses occurred between 1979 and 1985 in the region—nearly 30,000 workers lost work during that period alone. Of course, a recession in the early 1980s and increased foreign and domestic competition played a part as well, but the automation of the mills was perhaps the biggest factor in creating up to a 16 percent unemployment rate in the area.[21]

As with any wave in new technology, the overall trend in high-labor industries favors automation-centric employers. More recently, more than 300,000 jobs vanished from the steel industry from 1990 through 2017. The prevailing view is that employers employ automation to improve productivity: more production per worker over time. "The basic story is that one person can produce a lot more metal today than he or she could produce a few decades ago," notes Gary Burtless, an economist with the Brookings Institution.[22]

Christine Walley, an MIT anthropologist whose father lost his job at Wis-consin Steel, has studied the steelworking community of the Calumet region and the economic displacement of local, semi-, and unskilled workers. She notes that society has done an inadequate job of helping those thrown out of work from automation, which is moving hard and fast into every office.

"As automation—increasingly powered by artificial intelligence—continues its steady march, she (Walley) thinks white-collar workers will begin to confront the same displacement and anxiety blue-collar workers have faced to decades," notes Elizabeth Svoboda.[23]

When I saw Derrick Smith about a year ago, I didn't initially know that he had worked at Wisconsin Steel. Only after a casual conversation in front of my local supermarket did I learn that he never fully recovered from that job loss. He had been hauling scrap in the tough interim years and was ringing a bell for the Salvation Army. Were the steelworkers of 30 or 40 years ago like the most vulnerable workers of *today*? Do they think that the overall trend of capital investment into automation won't impact them or believe it is some kind of rogue wave? Are today's workers blind to the tsunami of automation?

CLOSER TO HOME: A WHITE-COLLAR EXAMPLE OF MASSIVE JOB LOSSES

For thousands of curious minds since the printing press was introduced in the fifteenth century, journalism—and most forms of writing for that matter—offered a way to earn a living without much, if any, formal training. You didn't need to pass an exam, get a certificate, or even get a degree in journalism to launch a career in newspapers, magazines, or book publishing. Is it a profession, craft, or trade? You'll spark a heated debate exploring this topic.

What you can't deny is that publishing, throughout history, has been labor intensive in a way that was ripe for automation. From cutting down trees, paper mills, giant printing presses to legions of reporters and editors around the globe, hundreds of thousands of professionals made a living putting words on paper, although it took a lot of people to produce a book, magazine, or newspaper. Big newspapers—there were several in each large city— had their own trucking fleets and distribution networks from newsstands to paperboys (that's how I got my start in the business). News and features were delivered on your front doorstep or in your mailbox. Thousands of hands touched the final product before it was delivered directly to you. It wasn't a particularly efficient process—hundreds of hands touched newspapers before they reached your doorstep—but it was profitable for hundreds of years to do it this way.

Newspapers and magazines were brimming with advertising during their best years. "Display" and classified (for newspapers) advertising, of course, paid the bills and the salaries of reporters, editors, and production specialists from printing press operators to top editors, who often enjoyed six-figure salaries and global prestige. Profits rolled in from hundreds of pages of ads on everything from hamburgers to high fashion.

The Internet and digital publishing changed most of that business model. From blogs to e-books and digital newspapers, you no longer needed printing presses, distribution supply chains, or even trees. One computer could supply nearly all of your prepress production needs. The World Wide Web provided global distribution—again, mostly for free. It was hard for a print newspaper to compete with news sources from anywhere that could be produced and delivered for virtually nothing. If you had an Internet address (URL), you could put anything from a recipe to an investigative piece in front of the world.

The commoditization of news, features, and information made huge editorial staffs difficult to justify; suddenly *anyone* could become a publisher with little or no labor or production costs. So the massive network of news bureaus and expensive editorial offices in Manhattan skyscrapers was downsized dramatically—a trend that continues and has directly impacted those in the industry (see my preface if you need to refresh your memory).

The decline in publishing employment, though, took a double hit. Not only did technology make production costs virtually disappear, advertising that once paid the bulk of a publisher's bills began to be vacuumed by automated advertising platforms run by Amazon, Google, and Facebook (among other online entities). Why pay a newspaper or magazine thousands of dollars to imprecisely target their readers when you could *precisely* find likely customers who already said they would "like" your product or service, which was the work of robots and algorithms and not a human marketing department?

The employment drain is hardly over as digital publishing, mobile applications and paper-free media eat at traditional media and its traditional sources of revenue such as display/classified advertising and subscriptions. Why run a printing plant when you can instantaneously see the latest news on your phone for free?

HOW KNOWLEDGE WORKERS CAN PROSPER

As noted earlier, we're in the midst of an epic downsizing of the conventional labor force. Workers will need to be more, well, *human*, to survive the automation age. According to a World Economic Forum (WEF) report entitled "The Future of Jobs," public education and private employers need to find people who are broadly educated and multidisciplinary.[24]

"Overall, social skills—such as persuasion, emotional intelligence and teaching others—will be in higher demand across industries than narrow technical skills," the WEF study stated. "In essence, technical skills will need to be supplemented with strong social and collaboration skills."[25]

It's not enough to have a narrow skill set. You'll need to know and do more. Back to my example on the publishing industry: The number of jobs lost in this business forces a hard look at structural changes that are unlikely to be reversed, particularly in labor-intensive operations. The double whammy of online production cost savings and automated advertising, which went into full swing following the financial crisis and recession of 2007–2009, took its greatest toll on newspaper employment. From 2008 through 2017, reports Pew Research, newspaper newsroom employment fell 45 percent. When the 2008 stock market crash hit, more than 70,000 were employed in newsrooms. Now it's less than 40,000. While digital newsroom employment increased 79 percent during that period, there are still less than 15,000 workers in that subindustry, so tens of thousands of editorial employees lost their jobs.[26]

What happened in publishing? Automation changed the cost curve. A combination of cheap technology and a pronounced elimination of labor merged with a massive degree of automation. In this case, online giants like Google were able to employ "bots" to find potential advertisers and direct them to the appropriate kind of advertising and potential customers with a high degree of precision. That's because of the extensive data mining and analysis online companies do every time you're online or use your mobile device. They collect and store data on what you search for, what you click on, and where you go—online and outside of your home. They know what restaurants you patronize, the merchandise you buy, and even the images you post. It wouldn't be hard to conclude that they know more about your consumption habits than you do. Algorithms then complete the task of connecting you with advertising by popping up screen ads of things you have bought or *may* buy. They know where you go and even what you look like. I hate to say Big Brother is watching you, but *Big Data* certainly is!

The bots are trying to read your mind and often to get you to purchase something else. That's why they've led to the unemployment of hundreds of thousands of workers. Yet the bots aren't going to be confined to targeted advertising. The companies that employ bots, keep in mind, are not interested in creating new jobs, they are interested in new *profits*.

WHY WORKERS SUCCUMB TO AUTOMATION

While steelmaking and publishing are two good examples, the larger story is the *integration* of automated production, artificial intelligence (AI)/machine learning, distribution, and data mining into even larger, more complex tasks and industries.

As machines get "smarter"—that is, through artificial intelligence they can do more demanding work—they will make even more jobs obsolete. That means it will be cheaper for a machine to do what a human did because an AI program won't demand time off, overtime, health insurance, and a pension. It's simple economics.

The overall truth in the thinking machine age is that if a program can take over a basic human task, it will happen—once it becomes cost effective. Here's an overview of industries that downsized employment over the past century, according to the BLS (U.S. Bureau of Labor Statistics):[27]

Table 1.1   Key Industries That Have Experienced Long-Term Job Losses

Industry	Peak Employment Year/Jobs	Current State
Apparel	1973/2.4 million	−86% since 1990
Mining & Logging	1981/1.3 million	in decline
Manufacturing	1979/20 million (approx.)	AI/auto. integration
Information*	2001/4 million (approx.)	still downsizing

*The BLS includes publishing and telecommunications (hardwired phone services in particular) in this overly broad category.

Note: This survey covers an overview of industries from 1939 through 2015. I've included cyclical industries such as construction and energy to better reflect long-term trends.

This view of a handful of the hardest-hit industries, of course, doesn't tell the whole story. For some reason, the BLS combines conventional publishing with telecommunications in one category, although these industries couldn't be more different. Publishing employment declined because of advertising and production automation, as noted in the previous section. The telecommunications industry, which includes legacy companies like AT&T and regional spin-offs, downsized significantly because millions of customers switched from copper-wire landlines to wireless phones, cable, and satellite connections. There was other considerable consolidation: the original AT&T monopoly ("Ma Bell") was broken up into regional operating companies, then reassembled as a gargantuan telecom giant over time.

Mining and logging, it should be noted, weren't necessarily downsized due to automation, although it plays a part. Mining needed fewer workers because in the case of coal, mining machines became much larger and needed fewer operators. Coal mining also shifted from shafts deep in the mountains of Appalachia to much less costly surface mining in the Powder River Basin in Wyoming in recent decades. Here again, significantly less labor was needed to mine more coal, which could be scraped from relatively accessible veins near the ground. The advent of "fracking" technology in the energy industry made more oil and gas accessible without resorting to expensive ocean derricks. Much of that process is machine driven, of course, and is ongoing.

Apparel, as most labor economists have observed, involved a massive shift of labor from the United States and textile mills in the Appalachian Piedmont to factories in Asia, particularly China, where the cost of labor was dramatically cheaper. While some of that production was automated— and continues to be mass-produced—the labor savings moved much of that work offshore.

What these diverse industries have in common is that their methods of production are continuing to be reshaped by technology, with automation and AI playing a powerful role in further lowering costs.

THE MOST VULNERABLE PROFESSIONS AND JOBS: GENERAL TRENDS

Here's one rule for the thinking machine age: Digital systems are much better handling massive amounts of data and doing relatively straightforward, routine things. They can handle processing your online purchase to make sure the warehouse sends out the right merchandise overnight. Robots can also build simple things—and are often able to fix themselves. Machines can write press releases and articles. If there's a formula or algorithm involved—and it doesn't involve complex cognitive skills—it can be automated.

Here's where the automation trend is headed:

1) **Manufacturing Is Going to Continue to Be Automated, only on a Much Larger, Smarter Scale.** Industrial robot sales broke a record in 2018, adding to more than 250,000 installed machines worldwide, according to the Robotics Industries Association.[28] As companies discover how to integrate robots into more manufacturing operations— this is happening across the world—they will install more robots, which are also becoming more cost effective and able to do more tasks.

2) **Nonmanufacturing Industries Will Use More Robots.** Traditionally, robots have been most extensively used in assembly lines, most notably in vehicle plants. Some 88 percent of factory jobs lost since 2000, reports a recent Ball State study, were due to automation, not foreign outsourcing.[29] Robots don't need a pension, healthcare, union representation or cost-of-living raises. Robots are being used in nonautomotive applications. For example, robotic surgery is increasingly used in hospital surgeries, where a surgeon manipulates a robotic arm. According to the Robotics Industries Association, "non-automotive robot orders increased as well with life sciences (184%), plastics/rubber (100%), and metals (three percent) leading the way."[30]

3) **Transportation Will Be Disrupted by Driverless Vehicles.** Machine disruption has a steep human price, though. If the robotic car gains wide acceptance, for example, it may eventually displace something like 200,000 taxi drivers and chauffeurs, who make an average $12 an hour, according to the U.S. Bureau of Labor Statistics.[31] Everything from decent-paying truck driving to middle-management jobs will be eliminated. That endangers nearly 2 million truck drivers, who earn a median income of $42,000 annually, and 800,000 delivery truck drivers.[32] Will drones and robotic vehicles displace more than 3 million drivers all at once? It's unlikely, but it's a trend that's worth watching closely.

4) **Anything Repetitive and Formulaic Will Be Automated.** This includes any task from filling out forms to company earnings reports. If it can be replicated a million times—and it's just a matter of inserting data—machines will be able to do it. That means anyone writing basic reports that don't require extensive analysis will be threatened by machine learning. Keep in mind that spreadsheets and databases are being generated by programs. Even legal forms handled by lawyers and paralegals are being automated.

5) **Market Traders and Most Financial Service Professions Are Archaic.** It wasn't too long ago that you could get a job on a stock or commodities exchange and trade just by yelling out prices on a noisy, crowded trading floor. That job has long since gone the way of the buggy whip. Algorithmic or high-frequency trading moves at the speed of light. Case in point: I got a tour of the Chicago Mercantile Exchange when I first started to research this book. The size of a football field, it contained data screens for prices on commodity contracts from corn

to pork bellies. The exchange, along with its cousin the Chicago Board of Trade, had been in existence for more than a century. Then "program" trading came along, where computers would see all of the current prices and execute the best trade in seconds. At that point, humans had no advantage and nearly every one of the trading "pits" closed, making the trading floor a museum exhibit. Several of my neighbors, sadly, who had made a good living lost their jobs. Goldman Sachs reported in 2017, for example, that it had replaced 600 stock traders with 200 computer engineers.[33] When a machine can see all prices through an electronic exchange—and make trades in a fraction of a second—humans will be left to evaluate the big picture of markets and economies, although machines are catching up on that front as well. The overall picture, it's important to note, is not positive for the financial services industry as a whole. Online programs are assembling personalized portfolios, so that threatens money managers, financial planners, and brokers. Nearly any financial product can be bought on the Internet directly, even insurance, so that is forcing insurance brokers and agents into other lines of work. Even bookkeepers and accountants are threatened. Anything to do with money, numbers, and markets involves tons of data that can be better sorted, analyzed, and traded upon by programs. Humans, however, will have an important role as gatekeepers for all of this machine knowledge, as we'll see in future chapters.

6) **Middle Management Will Be Increasingly Outsourced to Machines.** Any task that requires large amounts of data analysis can be better handled by thinking machines. Looking at sales trends and want to present the latest information in a power point? It's being automated. Trying to understand which products are most profitable in your company's extensive offerings? Machine learning is taking that task over. How many jobs are imperiled by the growing ability of machines to sort through ever more complex reams of data? It's hard to say, but this is a frontier that is being breached as back offices and middle management are being automated.

7) **Professional Expertise Is No Longer the Exclusive Domain of Professionals.** Machines can read X-rays and make diagnoses based on evaluating images. Robots can perform basic surgical procedures. Programs can complete legal forms and briefs. Doctors, lawyers, accountants, money managers, writers/journalists, publishing professionals, and even artists are competing with machines.

I know this sounds bleak, but much of the automation trend is not only happening now, it will blindside those are not prepared for it. For most, it's like being a frog in boiling water. We don't know we're in trouble until we're parboiled.

Shelly Palmer, CEO of the Palmer Group, which specializes in technology solutions, has this sobering observation:

> First, technological progress is neither good nor bad; it just is. There's no point in worrying about it, and there is certainly no point trying to add some narrative about the "good ol' days." It won't help anyone. The good news is that we know what's coming. All we have to do is adapt. . . . We know that machine learning is going to be used to automate many, if not most, low-level cognitive tasks. Our goal is to use our high-level cognitive ability to anticipate what parts of our work will be fully automated and what parts of our work will be so hard for machines to do that man-machine partnership is the most practical approach."[34]

Adaptation and a focus on uniquely human skills is an antidote to this dystopian picture. Those ideas will be explored in depth in future chapters.

FINAL NOTES

If there's a bright side to the onslaught of automation, one could argue that it's saved lives because plant floors have become safer. No longer do steelworkers have to be exposed to the perils of molten steel. Assembly-line workers don't have to worry about being injured simply due to repetitive fatigue. Mindless jobs are being automated so that humans can use their brains and brawn for better things, perhaps even to enjoy a better life.

Now a greater concern is the impact of automation on the larger labor force. As devices that replace human labor—often dangerous or repetitive tasks—robots are doing everything from plowing fields to making autos. (Racine-based Case IH recently introduced a driverless tractor that will use GPS, radar, and cameras to navigate farm fields across the heartland.)

Although automation and outsourcing will continue to ravage the job market for underskilled workers (see chapter 3 for more detail on job losses), the upside is that systems tied into human-machine interfaces will create new jobs, but will require workers who can effectively cross boundaries from technology to the arts and are skilled in communication and collaboration.

Of course, that raises the question: How can society successfully navigate this ongoing mash-up of automation technologies if millions of semiskilled—and eventually college-educated—workers can't find sustainable, meaningful employment? Which jobs are most at risk—now and in the future? In the next chapter, I will examine this question in more detail.

THREE

The Bad News: Jobs That Will Go the Way of the Dodo

As the last chapter explained, entire industries and tasks are imperiled. In this chapter, I will look deeper into the vocational divide and explore which jobs are most at risk.

If you want to get an overview of an entire industry or set of trends, it's often best to talk to a mutual fund or money manager. They are paid handsomely to look at the big picture, assemble a portfolio of stocks and bonds, and hope they can make money for their investors. Travis Briggs, for example, is the CEO of ROBO Global, which created the first index concentrated on global robotics, automation, and artificial intelligence companies. The ROBO ETF, listed in the United States, tracks this index and invests in the leading companies in the automation age. An ETF (exchange-traded fund) is like a mutual fund that pools investors' money, only it's listed on the stock exchange. The ROBO Global group, with more than $3 billion in fund assets under management that track the firm's indices worldwide, researches the most promising stocks in artificial intelligence, automation, logistics, manufacturing, sensing, and related technologies. It's Briggs's job to have the "30,000-foot view" of 12 automation-related subindustries.[35]

"We will have to rethink what jobs will look like," Briggs told me, based on what he's seeing. "Routine jobs will be replaced. Data is the electricity of the 21st century. The next evolution will be digitally driven. There will be a marriage between data and physical machines."[36]

To gain a deeper understanding of Briggs's prediction, you have to enter into a portfolio manager's thinking. They are always trying to predict which companies will grow their earnings well into the future. To make those kinds of decisions, portfolio managers have to make educated guesses on which enterprises have the best technologies, management, and applications for the future. But first, some definitions of what Briggs is considering when he vets the best companies in automation:

- **Manufacturing and Industrial Automation.** These are the most-used applications, which have been dominated by single-task "robot arms," which are evolving to do more sophisticated tasks on the factory floor.

- **Logistics Automation.** This technology moves goods from one place to another and broadly ranges from warehouse robots that move merchandise to self-driving trucks.

- **Health Care.** Some surgeries are being done through robotic machines. More applications are being developed, including better use of digitized medical records to prevent medical errors.

- **Food & Agriculture.** Once the most labor-intensive industry, human labor is greatly reduced by devices like driverless robotic tractors that use geographic positioning systems to more efficiently harvest crops, apply fertilizer and pesticides, and plant seeds.

- **Energy.** The aging electrical grid and other energy systems will be connected to "smart" systems that will better allocate energy to where it's needed around the world.

- **3D Printing.** Using software and polymers, this technology is being used to create everything from small toys to entire house frames. Say you enter a program into a computer using a 3D printer. It will essentially melt plastic into a three-dimensional shape, ranging from individual chess pieces to artificial limbs.

- **Security and Surveillance.** Using cameras and facial recognition, these systems can not only show you who's coming and going, it can identify individual faces.

- **AI.** As discussed earlier, these systems use machine learning to process and analyze "big" data sets to identify everything from consumer preferences to global climate change.

- **Sensing, Actuation, and Integration.** Using sensors and "machine vision," these systems can attempt to "see" specific objects, which is useful in everything from energy management to picking merchandise in a warehouse. Integration incorporates these abilities into a larger system.

In the automation world, the most compelling companies have the technology to either replace or augment human labor at a lower cost. And they will do it any number of ways. AI, for example, allows machines to sort through billions of bits of data to make decisions or to see patterns. Machine learning is part of that process. "Deep" machine learning takes it to a new level, where patterns are identified and integrated into other programs.[37]

THINK MORE ABOUT THE *TASKS* THAT WILL DISAPPEAR, NOT THE JOBS

The most immediate insight from looking at where automation is headed is that certain jobs that are relatively prevalent now will disappear—if you can make a prediction from the preceding section. If you're a warehouse worker, robots will eventually take over most of the work as they become smarter and cheaper. Security guards looking at cameras all day long may lose their jobs to systems that already know who should—and shouldn't—be entering building and secured areas. And farmers who once spent hours

---

SOME BRIEF DEFINITIONS

The reason jobs will be lost across many industries is that computer systems are much better at looking and sorting through *big data*, that is, massive amounts of information.

Predictive analytics is then employed to identify patterns and tell people what might happen based on what they are seeing from the programs they run. What are you likely to buy based on what you searched for on the Internet and what you've bought? Algorithms are constantly asking that question and trying to make you buy more.

Machine or computer vision complements big-data analysis to identify objects and faces (a feature of many smartphones). In a warehouse, how can a robot pick a book and not a brick to pack for shipping?

Integration means that a machine can use all of the above to sense and act upon data, analysis, and what it "sees." It will know the wrong thing to do and avoid mistakes, ideally.

Neural nets, modeled after the human brain, are the basic frameworks for processing all this information using different mounds of data and the ability to analyze it all. What's the difference between a peach and a baseball? When is someone frowning and not grimacing? That requires a tremendous amount of processing power that goes way beyond simple pattern recognition. Note: Since we don't completely understand how our brains work, this is the most challenging field in automation and AI.

AUTOMATION SNAPSHOT: THE JANITORIAL ROBOT

As long as anyone can remember, it took teams of workers hours to mop and sweep floors. It was—and is—a tedious task that paid little but employed a lot of people as commercial, retail, office, and industrial facilities got ever larger.

Machines that made the job go smoother certainly helped over the last century, but they needed someone to push and guide them, so while the time it took to clean a floor took less time, you still had to pay someone to do the task. Enter the robotic floor cleaner.

Ranging from small robotic vacuums to industrial-scale floor cleaners, robotic devices not only do the job without people, they know exactly where they are going. They employ sensors to tell them where they are and where they need to be, using AI and machine vision. It's as if they have spatial and visual sense to give them direction. They even have autonomous navigation systems.

The retail giant Walmart said it was deploying hundreds of robotic janitors in its stores by the end of January 2019. They will largely scrub floors, although they are unlikely to greet you with a smile at the door.[38]

---

in a tractor plowing, seeding, fertilizing, and harvesting vast acreage will employ robots and be able to monitor the whole process from their home computers. Of course, none of these technologies are in widespread use as I write this, although these trends are works in progress. In order for them to be widely adopted, they need to be "scaled up," that is, made affordable and efficient. You also need to focus on which tasks are most vulnerable.

AUTOMATION'S HIDDEN IMPACT

For economists, the automation wave is bound to increase productivity: producing more of something with less labor and associated costs. Industrial robots are meant to do just that. Instead of having three shifts of workers picking orders in a warehouse, for example, a team of robots can do it, thus reducing the labor cost for an employer. They just have to pay to buy, power, and maintain the robots.

Yet in terms of human labor loss, "the arrival of one industrial robot in a local labor market coincides with an employment drop of 5.6 workers," notes researchers Acemoglu and Restrepo.[39]

Automation has several effects on the labor market. It may displace the workers performing a particular job in a particular industry, leading to reduced employment opportunities and wages for workers who historically held such positions. However, other sectors and occupations may expand to soak up labor freed from the tasks performed by machines, and it is even possible that productivity gains due to new automation technologies may expand employment possibilities in the industries in which they are deployed.[40]

The takeaway from this observation is that automated jobs *may* lead to newer jobs. More skilled workers will need to program, maintain, and fix the robots. Will there be "smarter" workers employed to replace the basic labor jobs that were lost to automation? While it's unlikely, we'll explore in future chapters the skills needed to succeed in a robotic workplace. Also keep in mind that many robots are designed to work alongside human workers, so the future is a bit blurry.

What can't be denied is that automation has eliminated millions in jobs in the most vulnerable industries. While some of those workers lost out due to imported goods and globalization, job loss was most pronounced where simple tasks could be automated.

An important study by Michael Hicks and Srikant Devaraj of Ball State University concluded that "almost 88 percent of job losses in manufacturing in recent years can be attributable to productivity growth, and the long-term changes to manufacturing employment are mostly linked to the productivity of American factories."[41] The researchers take their inquiry a step further and estimate how many jobs were unfilled if productivity remained static from 2010. In short, they were asking the question, "how many people *weren't* hired because factories were automated." Here is a summary of that part of their research:

Table 2 Jobs Not Filled Due to Productivity and Automation

Industry	Jobs Lost
Durable goods manufacturing	8.1 million
Computer/Electronics products	4 million
Nondurable goods manufacturing	2.2 million
Motor vehicles bodies/trailers/parts	586,000
Chemical products	426,000

Note: "Durable goods" are things that have a long shelf life like appliances and machine tools.[42]

AUTOMATION SNAPSHOT: CHATBOTS THAT
LISTEN AND TAKE ACTION

One of the most popular outgrowths of automation and AI are "chatbots," which respond to human commands on search engines, phones, and "smart speakers." You can essentially use natural language to ask these auto-servants to find anything from a popular term to the latest weather forecast.

Chatbots are employed as Siri in Apple iPhones, Cortana in Microsoft products, Google Assistant, and Alexa in Amazon's smart speaker. What they do is replace the need to type in a search. They respond to your voice and figure out (most of the time, at least) what you want to do. Although they are far from perfect, they take over for people who used to operate customer service lines. While not suited for complex tasks—like doing your taxes or figuring out your cable or phone bill—they are designed to add a human element to an automated feature.

"Bots will change how customer service is delivered," note researchers Anastassia Lauterbach and Andrea Bonime-Blanc. "The use of chatbots by companies in the financial and healthcare industries will save a collective $22 billion in time and salaries by 2022, according to Juniper Research."[43]

Hoping to have a steady career in customer service? You will probably have to look elsewhere for job stability.

All told, Hicks and Devaraj estimate that from 8 to 12 million jobs went unfilled simply because the manufacturing processes across the industries they studied became more efficient. While not all of that was due to automation, it's clear that any basic tasks on any production line that are repetitive and more efficiently accomplished by a robotic system are going to be machine operated—if the economics make sense for a company. Even those skills that involve a degree of basic communication are on the chopping block. They involve "bots" that respond to requests for information.

INTEGRATION IS THE KEY

It's not easy to make simple conclusions about job losses that are caused by automation. Installing robotic systems requires significant capital investment, and those expenditures have to pay for themselves in measurable labor-cost reductions. In some cases, humans cost less than robots. Then there's the problem of integration. Robots may not work well with the systems companies already have in place. They may be costly and incompatible with the way they do business. And some robots may only do one task, while "humanoid" robots may be employed to do a range of tasks from taking care of the elderly to monitoring security (think any Hollywood movie you've ever seen with robots in starring roles).

Complexity, of course, costs more money because robot manufacturers need to *integrate* a variety of tasks into a thinking machine. Consider a "domestic" humanoid robot that may attend older people who are home alone (they are being used in Japan). They not only need AI in their brain, they need machine vision to be able to spot someone when they fall or need help. They will need their eyes and ears to do their job—plus the ability to process what they are sensing. Ideally, they are replacing human caregivers, who understand and can serve the complex needs of frail older people. They are considered "humanoid," but are they up to doing more than providing simple services? Complexity in terms of a robot's intellect will take time.

It's reasonable to assume that simple, single-task, stationary robots will probably consume more jobs than multitasking bots, at least on the factory floor. According to the World Economic Forum:

> Robot adoption rates diverge significantly across sectors, with 37% to 23% of companies planning this investment, depending on industry. Companies across all sectors are most likely to adopt the use of stationary robots, in contrast to humanoid, aerial or underwater robots; however leaders in the Oil & Gas industry report the same level of demand for stationary and aerial and underwater robots, while employers in the Financial Services industry are most likely to signal the planned adoption of humanoid robots in the period up to 2022.[44]

Although the WEF report is generally optimistic on overall job growth in the future, it envisions a "new human-machine frontier within certain tasks." This translates to machines doing more analytical jobs that were once the province of administration, communications, consulting, and middle management. Here's a summary of what automation will mean in terms of less human labor:

- In 2018, an average of 71 percent of total task hours across the 12 industries covered in the report are performed by humans, compared to 29 percent by machines. By 2022, this average is expected to have shifted to 58 percent task hours performed by humans and 42 percent by machines.

- In terms of total working hours, no work task was yet estimated to be predominantly performed by a machine or an algorithm (in 2018). By 2022, this picture is projected to have somewhat changed, with machines and algorithms on average increasing their contribution to specific tasks by 57 percent.
- By 2022, 62 percent of organization's information and data processing and information search and transmission tasks will be performed by machines compared to 46 percent today.
- Even those work tasks that have thus far remained overwhelmingly human—communicating and interacting (23 percent); coordinating, developing, managing, and advising (20 percent); as well as reasoning and decision making (18 percent)—will begin to be automated (30 percent, 29 percent, and 27 percent respectively).
- Relative to their starting point today, the expansion of machines' share of work task performance is particularly marked in the reasoning and decision making, administering, and looking for and receiving job-related information tasks.[45]

Again, it's only fair to say that whatever tasks are automated should mesh with how people work and process information. Decision making, managing, and communications are still higher-order activities that are difficult to automate. There are myriad human factors that need to be explored.

WHICH JOBS ARE MOST IMPERILED?

The automation wave will spread far beyond hourly occupations into the office. Millions of hourly jobs in retail and basic services will also disappear, according to the Oxford study cited in the introduction. In a comprehensive review, the researchers sorted and ranked some 700 occupations according to their probability of being automated or "computerized" in their language. They made their evaluation based on existing and future technologies, the nature of the tasks (simple and generally repetitive), and how machines can use data to make decisions. Of course, this list is hardly a death knell for these occupations; companies may not choose to automate these tasks for various reasons.

Jobs on this list are ranked for their *high likelihood of being automated* based on the researchers' criteria. Nevertheless, if you're considering taking up one of these occupations, you shouldn't expect any job stability.

(Note: the researchers' original list ranked occupations least to most likely to be automated, so I'm starting at the bottom working my way up.)

MOST LIKELY TO BE AUTOMATED: 100 JOBS THAT ARE ENDANGERED[46]

1. Telemarketers
2. Title Examiners, Searchers
3. Hand Sewers
4. Math Technicians
5. Insurance Underwriters
6. Watch Repairers
7. Cargo/Freight Agents
8. Tax Preparers
9. Photographic Processors
10. New Accounts Clerks
11. Library Technicians
12. Data Entry Keyers
13. Timing Device Assemblers
14. Insurance Claims Clerks
15. Brokerage Clerks
16. Loan Clerks
17. Insurance Appraisers (Auto)
18. Sports Officials
19. Tellers
20. Etchers/Engravers
21. Packaging/Filling Machine Operators
22. Procurement Clerks
23. Shipping/Receiving Clerks
24. Milling/Planning Machine Operators
25. Credit Analysts
26. Parts Salespersons
27. Insurance Claims Adjusters

28. Driver/Sales Workers
29. Radio Operators
30. Legal Secretaries
31. Bookkeeping/Accounting Clerks
32. Inspectors
33. Models
34. Hosts/Hostesses
35. Credit Authorizers
36. Payroll Clerks
37. Agricultural Technicians
38. Telephone Operators
39. Real Estate Brokers
40. File Clerks
41. Counter/Rental Clerks
42. Prepress Technicians
43. Movie Projectionists
44. Camera Repairers
45. Cashiers
46. Ophthalmic Lab Technicians
47. Graders/Scalers
48. Pesticide Handlers
49. Grinding/Polishing Workers
50. Crushing/Polishing Machine Operators
51. Dental Lab Technician
52. Textile Bleaching/Dying Operators
53. Farm Labor Contractors
54. Electromechanical Equipment Assemblers
55. Shoe Machine Operators
56. Team Assemblers
57. Woodworking Machine Setters
58. Bridge and Lock Tenders

59. Billing/Posting Clerks
60. Ushers/Lobby Attendants/Ticket Takers
61. Restaurant Clerks
62. Fabric Menders
63. Gaming Dealers
64. Locomotive Engineers
65. Textile Machine Operators
66. Wood Model Makers
67. Surveyors
68. Secretaries/Administrative Assistants
69. Quarry Rock Splitters
70. Counter Attendants
71. Switchboard Operators
72. Compensation/Benefits Managers
73. Office Clerks
74. Receptionists
75. Dispatchers (except for emergency services)
76. Jewelers/Metal Workers
77. Postal Service Clerks
78. Landscaping/Groundskeeping Workers
79. Adhesive Bonding Machine Operators
80. Electrical/Electric Equipment Assemblers
81. Molding/Casting Machine Operators
82. Animal Breeders
83. Print/Binding Workers
84. Operating Engineers
85. Library Assistants
86. Gaming Surveillance
87. Nuclear Power Plant Operators
88. Bill Collectors
89. Textile Cutting Machine Operators

90. Weighers/Measurers/Samplers

91. Manicurists/pedicurists

92. Paralegals/Legal Assistants

93. Agricultural Inspectors

94. Janitorial Supervisors

95. Door-to-Door Sales Workers

96. Tire Builders

97. Hotel/Motel Desk Clerks

98. Painters/Paperhangers/Plasterers/Stucco Masons

99. Excavating Machine Operators

100. Short-order Cooks

What to make of this list, which is abbreviated from 700 occupations? There are some common traits: the simplest, most routine, manual tasks are within the realm of thinking machines. If there's little training or education needed, then that could be an instant red flag.

FINAL NOTES

Although the complete list from the Oxford study gets to be redundant, it's also full of conjecture: Which occupations will survive simply because companies want the *human touch* of a person at the front desk or dealing with customers? How many jobs will be retained because people are adding personal contact to interactions with clients or customers?

You also need to be discerning when looking at the Oxford list. Some of these jobs have already been highly automated or moved offshore, particularly those in low-value manufacturing (think textiles, electronic assembly, basic manufacturing). But that doesn't mean that workers who used to operate machine tools, for example, won't be needed—or employed. They may just be hired in smaller numbers and be required to have more math and computer coding skills.

Yet there are some specific truths in the Oxford study that are likely to prevail. Here are some key summary points:

Form-Oriented and Clerical Work Will Be Automated. These "back office" personnel are being replaced by computer systems. There's already been significant automation in the credit, mortgage, legal, and insurances industries. Anything to do with paperwork can be done much faster and efficiently by computer.

Front-Line/Back Office Services Are Mostly Going Away. Anyone who works at a "front" desk, teller window, or reception area is at risk, although this trend is moving slower than the clerical automation wave. Local banks, for example, used to have hundreds of employees. Now with ubiquitous ATMs, forms processing, and online/mobile banking applications, this is a job category that's shrinking fast. Clerks, tellers, administrative assistants, and basic paperwork handlers are most endangered.

Financial Services Are Ripe for Extensive Digitization. When you can go online and set up a mutual fund portfolio that's completely automated, why pay more for a broker-advisor? "Robo advisers" are now growing at an exponential rate. Anyone who's on the clerical or low-skilled end of this industry is imperiled.

Logistics Is Moving Fast into Robotics. Amazon is already pushing the automation transition hard with robotic stockers and "pickers" in their high-tech warehouses. When their automated supply chain system disrupts the majority of the retail industry—particularly grocery supply and distribution—more than 1 million jobs may be eliminated. Every industry that has to store or move anything is moving in this direction.

Any Basic Skill Will Be Done by a Machine. With computers behind nearly every manufacturing process, hands-on labor will be eliminated. You probably noticed the large number of pure-labor positions above can be done by machines, especially if those tasks are simple, repetitive, and don't require higher-level cognitive skills.

This is just a snapshot of what's already happening. The job-elimination trend will accelerate as artificial intelligence is merged with existing systems and drones. Yet there's reason to be optimistic. Certain kinds of work will lend itself to human-machine interaction. Innovation will come from this nexus of creativity, design, and collaboration. This promising intersection will be explored in the next chapter.

FOUR

Automate This! How Integrated Innovation Wins the Day

Although machines are getting really good at complex tasks such as coding, learning, and recognizing faces, the big ticket is what humans are uniquely suited to do: *innovation*. This chapter will feature some of the most compelling ideas. I'll also introduce the skills that are essential in this new age.

So far, you've seen a massive bank of dark clouds on the horizon. Millions of jobs will be automated, while millions may be created. How do you make sense of this brave new automation age? Let's review what we know and what's speculation.

The only sure thing in any scenario is that jobs will be eliminated or replaced. How many is up for debate. That leaves industry, nongovernmental bodies, and the public sector with the enormous social burden of either retraining or paying displaced workers a "universal income" (more on that later).

According to one estimate by the World Economic Forum, "reskilling" workers will cost some $34 billion—and that's based on a conservative estimate of retraining only 1.4 million employees.[47] The report predicts that 18 percent of those displaced by automation—about 250,000 people—will *not* be reskilled, so they will need some form of public assistance. That estimate seems incredibly low, however, based on all of the other studies I've seen.

Of course, with any prediction on long-term trends, the numbers could be way off on either end of the scale. The range is wide and prediction models can be faulty. On nearly the same day the WEF report was released, the

Washington think tank Brookings Institution concluded that the impact of AI alone would mean that manufacturing in America's heartland would be hardest hit, again triggering a need for massive retraining and public support.

"Repetitive tasks that involve processing information, performing physical activities or operating machinery will be the first to be replaced by artificial intelligence—which could hit manufacturing jobs hard," *The Washington Post* reported in reviewing the Brookings Study. "It's urgent. I think it's something Congress should have worked on yesterday," author Rob Maxim told the *Post*.[48] None of this, if you've been reading carefully, is much of a revelation. You need to dig a little deeper, though, to parse out how severe the automation jobs depletion wave is—and how we can prosper when it's in full swing.

Martin Ford, a Silicon Valley consultant and entrepreneur, was one of the first experts to warn of the automation job crisis. His best seller *Rise of the Robots: Technology and the Threat of a Jobless Future* (2015) was a five-alarm siren on the need to prepare for the tsunami of automation. He then followed up with *Architects of Intelligence*, which focuses more on AI. Unlike most researchers who examine the threats of AI and automation, Ford takes a more nuanced, economic view. He factors in ongoing issues like wage stagnation, an aging workforce, government indifference, and climate change impacts into his overall equations. While he lands in the same place that many academics advocate—a universal basic income for those uprooted by automation—his view is that long-term trends are going to accelerate automation, although no major societal institution is remotely prepared to deal with massive changes.

Pushing back against the common argument that college graduates— particularly those with technical, math, or science degrees—will prevail, Ford is skeptical about the degree to which STEM (science, technology, engineering, and math) education is the salve in the thinking machine age. The sheer number of graduates in these fields may exceed demand, particularly if the global economy is fundamentally slowing due to demographics (older folks consume less). This is his most cautious note about education and the future:

> It is becoming increasingly clear that a great many people will do all the right things in terms of pursuing an advanced education, but nonetheless fail to find a foothold in the economy of the future.[49]

Will we need creative biologists, engineers, and scientists to work on global problems ranging from desertification to water reclamation? Of course. But we also need to ask whether governments, politicians, and nongovernmental entities are fully committed to solving these life-threatening problems—and will marshal the political will and resources to tackle them. That's a concern in any time, but more of a barrier when isolationism and nationalism occupy center stage in any political arena. You can't think globally if you refuse to act locally.

Nevertheless, you need to cast a jaundiced eye that only proscribes one kind of skill or degree to be viable in the automation age. You'll need a diverse toolbox.

FORD'S FIVE VOCATIONAL SUGGESTIONS

Want to be less vulnerable in the automation age? You'll need to do what thinking machines aren't good at (yet). Ford makes these recommendations:

- **Avoid Jobs That Are Fundamentally Routine.** As we've discussed earlier, the more routine and repetitive a job is, the higher the likelihood that it can and will be automated (see our list in the previous chapter for occupations to avoid).

- **Creativity Is the Key.** If you can imagine, draw, design, or build something from scratch, you're ahead of the game. Sure, there are myriad computer programs that can do everything from animation to create blueprints for entire complexes, but someone has to have the vision for some groundwork and basic ideas. "Build something new," Ford suggests.

- **Mobility and Dexterity Are Important.** Many, if not most, robots will be stationary. They will stay in one place on the factory floor or remain embedded in software. But what if you have to move around to do different tasks? These two traits favor tradespeople like plumbers and electricians, who have to go on-site to figure out and fix problems.

- **Designed-Based Education Is Essential.** While computers will eventually learn how to program themselves—throwing millions of computer programmers out of work—Ford recommends that people take coding classes. At the very least, you'll need to know how machines "think." That's a building block for understanding whole systems and how you can help build better ones.

- **Human Skills Are Integral.** Yes, you'll still need the different forms of intelligence to do well (more on those later, of course). But the key to surviving in the automation age is the ability to integrate them with machine skills. Health-care professionals, for example, will need to understand digitized records systems and robotic surgical assistants. "Individual integration," Ford adds, "doesn't scale. Sometimes you need a person to be there."*

* Ford, 12/19/18 telephone interview. https://mforcfuture.com/about

ANOTHER VIEW: THE PROFIT MOTIVE THAT
PROPELS AUTOMATION

There is clearly another motive behind automation that I haven't dis-cussed in much detail: profit. Every executive and investor knows that if you can reduce a company's human labor costs, that grows the bottom line in a big way. When there are "reductions in force" or "rightsizing" or "down-sizing," that means operating expenses fall. Shareholders and investors rally around the higher profits, which translates into higher stock prices and loftier executive compensation.

Martin Ford and other critics of corporate and economic nationalism are deeply skeptical about who will profit the most. This revisits a question I posed earlier: Will millions of workers actually be retrained on a mass scale? Who will pay for the billions of dollars needed for reeducation or reskilling? Are they fully disclosing their strategic plans to integrate AI into automation systems? Will more new jobs really emerge to replace the occu-pations automated out of existence?

Troubling questions, to be sure. If you're caught in the automation mael-strom, it would be helpful to embrace the view that there isn't a great deal of transparency in the corporate realm on the degree to which automation will eliminate jobs.

At the 2019 World Economic Forum in Davos, Switzerland, world lead-ers and elite capitalists gathered to hear keynotes about global trends. It ranges from the glamorous (Bono usually attends) to the mundane (eco-nomic forecasts), but typically offers a host of ideas about the present and future. Davos guru Klaus Schwab, who has been championing the idea of a "Fourth Industrial Revolution" that unites data, machines, the Internet, and people, has consistently remarked that this sea change in labor will create more jobs than it destroys. Yet what if he's underplaying the reality? After all, no executive wants to brazenly trumpet that he's going to replace thousands of jobs with robots for the sake of improved profits.

Kevin Roose, who covers technology for *The New York Times*, went behind the scenes at Davos and found another narrative lurking behind the glossy WEF picture:[50]

All over the world, executives are spending billions of dollars to trans-form their businesses into lean, digitized, highly automated opera-tions. They crave the fat profit margins automation can deliver, and they see AI as a golden ticket to savings, perhaps by letting them whittle departments with thousands of workers down to just a few dozen.

Are companies being openly honest about the degree to which they are seeking to automate a large number of jobs? If so, the WEF forecasts—many of which I include in this book—are soft-pedaling the future. As with all predictions, please take them with a grain of salt.

Doubtless, companies have been dipping their toes into the automation water for decades. Yet it's only within the past decade or so that AI and machine learning have entered the picture in a significant way. Instead of investing millions just in stationery robots, AI is much cheaper to employ in nearly every company operation. Still, the investment dollars in AI and automation speak for themselves, according to Roose:[51]

- A 2017 survey by Deloitte found that 53 percent of companies had already started to use machines to perform tasks previously done by humans. The figure is expected to climb to 72 percent by next year.

- IBM's "cognitive solutions" unit, which uses AI to help businesses increase efficiency, has become the company's second-largest division, posting $5.5 billion in revenue last quarter (fourth quarter of 2018).

- The investment bank UBS projects that the AI industry could be worth as much as $180 billion by next year.

- Terry Gou, the chairman of the Taiwanese electronics manufacturer Foxconn, has said the company plans to replace *80 percent* of its workers with robots in the next five to 10 years.

What's important to keep in mind is that the natural trajectory for the global economy isn't altruism, it's *capitalism*. It's an amoral system at best. Companies have no embedded obligations to retrain workers who lose their jobs—unless governments force them to do so. So any assumption that displaced workers will be taken care of and repurposed for equal- or higher-paying jobs is a myth. That's why you need to keep a keen focus on the skills and education needed to prosper and not the forecasts or pronouncements by corporate elites.

QUAD I PROFESSIONS: NOT LIKELY TO BE AUTOMATED SOON (OXFORD STUDY LIST)

There are plenty of reasons to get excited about combining innovation, insight, and integration in any vocation. For starters, innovation is still the province of human creativity, which is chaotic, often intuitive, and doesn't always rely on data sets. Sometimes, it just happens. Merging *innovation* with machine *integration* makes sense because it utilizes what computers do best with uniquely human skills.

Although machines are certainly able to "learn" through sorting through mountains of data, they may not have the serendipitous powers to seize the moment of a new invention. They may not be able to *improvise*—the fourth "I"—to a degree necessary to handle ambiguous changes, like a seriously injured person in an emergency room (more on improvisation later).

Nikola Tesla, for example, envisioned alternating current by drawing a sketch in sand in a park in Budapest. He was taking a walk at the time—and quoting Goethe's *Faust* from memory. What does epic German poetry have to do with electrical engineering? Perhaps nothing directly, but Tesla's brain integrated the two different streams of thought to come up with a technology that he could *see*—and it changed the world.

To innovation and integration, I would add this human element: *insight*. Sometimes insight comes in "aha" or "eureka" revelations, while it also may come in the form of patterns no one else has seen. While you can certainly argue that machines can see and act upon data patterns, will they know what to do with them?

So the most promising positions in the thinking machine age are "I"-oriented roles. They may not even have the titles we give workers now. They may be "thought analysts" or "data inspiration specialists." And using today's nomenclature, they even may sound relatively boring. The World Economic Forum, in predicting which jobs will dominate in 2022, generated this short list:[52]

EMERGING JOBS

1. Data Analysts/Scientists
2. AI Specialists
3. General Operations Managers
4. Software Applications Developers
5. Sales/Marketing Professionals
6. Big Data Specialists
7. Digital Transformation Specialists

8. New Technology Specialists
9. Organizational Development Specialists
10. Information Technology Services

While there are few surprises in this WEF ranking, it deserves some pointed criticism: most of these jobs are *already* emerging professions as I write this, and have been for several years. It's not a stretch to conclude that most of them will *still* be important in an age of hyper-automation. Most of them also overlap. Who won't be involved with data or digital transformation? And AI and information technology are already ubiquitous in every modern organization.

The outlier in this sampling (again) are sales and marketing professionals, ironically, which made the Oxford ranking of most endangered. Why is there a contradiction? Although some sales jobs will be automated or eliminated, you will still need highly trained professionals to explain *what* they are selling—especially if what you're offering are complex services. Again, the human touch comes into play. Many decision makers want someone in a room telling them what they are hearing or buying. Sure, we make billions of simple transactions through machines every day, but some products and services aren't that easy to sell directly.

Then there's *improvisation*, the ability to assess a situation and try something new on the spot—something not contained in an algorithm. It's a uniquely human skill as I write this. So being a Quadruple I person makes you even more valuable in the age of automation.

WHAT ARE THE CHANCES YOUR JOB *WON'T* BE QUADRUPLE I IN NATURE?

As we've explored in the previous chapter, the more repetitive and form-oriented a job is, the more machines can take it over. But which jobs best combine the Quadruple I characteristics that I've described? I again turn to the Oxford study, which, although it's a few years old, still provides what I consider to be some fairly reliable guidelines on the best jobs to have in the automation age.

Please note: As with the other lists in this book, none of these jobs are *guaranteed*, only highly likely to survive under the Oxford parameters due to their relatively complex nature and difficulty in automating.

QUAD I JOBS THAT PROBABLY WON'T BE AUTOMATED SOON[53]

1. Recreational Therapists
2. Supervisors of Mechanics, Installers, and Repairers
3. Emergency Management (911 Centers) Directors
4. Mental Health/Substance Abuse Workers/Therapists
5. Audiologists
6. Occupational Therapists
7. Orthotists/Prosthetists
8. Health-care Social Workers
9. Oral Surgeons
10. First Responder Supervisors
11. Dietitians/Nutritionists
12. Lodging Managers
13. Choreographers
14. Sales Engineers
15. Physicians/Surgeons
16. Instructional Coordinators (teachers)
17. Psychologists
18. Dentists
19. Elementary School Teachers
20. Medical Scientists (except epidemiologists)
21. Education Administrators (principals, superintendents)
22. Podiatrists
23. Clinical/Counseling/School Psychologists
24. Mental Health Counselors
25. Fabric/Apparel Patternmakers
26. Set and Exhibit Designers
27. Human Resource Managers
28. Recreation Workers
29. Training/Development Managers

30. Speech Language Pathologists
31. Computer Systems Analysts
32. Social/Community Services Managers
33. Curators (museum)
34. Athletic Trainers
35. Medical/Health Services Managers
36. Preschool Teachers
37. Farm/Management Advisors
38. Anthropologists/Archaeologists
39. Special Education Teachers (secondary school)
40. High School Teachers
41. Clergy
42. Foresters
43. Guidance/Vocational Counselors
44. Career/Technical Education High School Teachers
45. Registered Nurses
46. Rehabilitation Counselors
47. Teachers and Instructors (other)
48. Forensic Science Technicians
49. Makeup Artists (theatrical)
50. Marine Engineers/Naval Architects
51. Educational Administrators
52. Mechanical Engineers
53. Pharmacists
54. Logistics Experts
55. Microbiologists
56. Organizational Psychologists
57. Coaches/Athletic Scouts
58. Sales/Marketing Managers
59. Hydrologists
60. Marriage/Family Therapists

61. Engineers (all other)
62. Training/Development Specialists
63. First-Line Administrative Supervisors
64. Biologists
65. Fund-raising Managers
66. Multimedia artists/animators
67. Computer Scientists
68. Chief Executives
69. Preschool/Childcare Administrators
70. Music Directors/Composers
71. Supervisors of Production and Operating Workers
72. Securities, Commodities Sales Agents
73. Conservation/Environmental Scientists
74. Middle School Special Education Teachers
75. Chemical Engineers
76. Architectural/Engineering Managers
77. Aerospace Engineers
78. Natural Sciences Managers
79. Environmental Engineers
80. Architects
81. Physical Therapist Assistants
82. Civil Engineers
83. Health Diagnostic Practitioners
84. Soil/Plant Scientists
85. Materials Scientists
86. Materials Engineers
87. Fashion Designers
88. Physical Therapists
89. Photographers
90. Producers/Directors
91. Interior Designers
92. Orthodontists

93. Art Directors
94. Supervisors of Corrections Officers
95. Religious Education Directors
96. Electrical Engineers
97. Biochemists/Biophysicists
98. Chiropractors
99. Occupational Therapy Assistants
100. Child, Family, and School Social Workers

This is a daunting list, to be sure. There are a few categories, however, that need to be highlighted, which reflect overall societal trends that will not be impacted by automation to as high a degree.

- **Aging and Hands-on Services Will Flourish.** First, one powerful trend that I haven't discussed is the aging of the American population—and most industrialized countries. As people get older, they need an array of services, most of which are best delivered directly by humans. "High-touch" professionals include therapists of all kinds, health-care workers, and dentists. While many of these growing occupations may be on the low end of the pay scale, the more education and experience you have, the better.

- **Psychological Support Services Will Be Needed.** What the Oxford study and subsequent reports don't discuss in much detail is the need for psychological support when the automation age claims an increasing number of jobs. Vocational and guidance counselors on all levels will be in high demand, along with therapists and substance-abuse counselors. Displaced workers will need a lot of help adjusting, and that will involve a full range of mental health services. Whether those services will be widely available—or provided—is another question.

- **Environmental Science Will Take Front Row.** Climate change and its multiple complex impacts will create growing demand for everyone from environmental engineers to hydrologists (more on this later). As we've seen in recent years, precipitation may be catastrophic in some areas and absent in others, leading to more flooding, wildfires, and agricultural disruption. Biologists and any scientists who understand these systemic changes will be sought after.

- **Engineers, Scientists, and Designers Will Still Be in Demand.** There's no doubt that the lion's share of the design process could be automated, but you still need people to identify and solve problems. Nearly every kind of engineer made this list, but they will need to be fluent in the Quad I paradigm. How can they integrate with the best technologies? How can they tackle uniquely human problems like over-population and resource depletion? Their insights will depend on how they see the world and can suggest possible solutions.

- **Creatives Will Still Be Needed.** Sure, computers are composing music and "making" art. But we will still need new Beethovens, Hemingways, Picassos, and St. Laurents to break the mold of conformity and cultural stagnation. We will still need Rosalind Franklins to discern crystalline structures to see DNA and Jane Addams types to innovate social services. Movies will still need to be written, acted in, and produced. Novels will still be written offering unique insights into our malaise and future. The visual arts will be needed more than ever, along with dance, theatre, and other performing arts. We discover our humanity through the arts, something we'll need to revisit even more often in the automation age.

- **Teaching Will Never Be More Important.** We will need to learn new things in school and throughout our lives. Lifelong learning will become the new norm. That means an even greater demand for good teachers on every level and those who supervise them and design coursework. Will schools and universities remain in their current form? Probably not, as some learning will go online. But talented teachers will always be needed to instruct humans on complex subjects and cater to those with vocational dislocation and special needs.

FINAL NOTES

There is no perfect view of the future, mostly because there are so many wild cards at play. How many jobs will be automated and how many will be retained because they involve hands-on interaction with machines and humans? The only guarantees are that human behavior, health, and creativity will continue to be complicated. We don't fully understand human nature now, so how will we expect machines to deal directly with our myriad needs?

The next chapter will explore how we can leverage our tremendous social skills to form networks and collaborate.

FIVE

The Social Labor Ecosystem: How Worker Collaboration Can Revolt against the Robots

What a lot of machines can't do effectively—at least not today—is to have improvised, quirky, collaborative brainstorms. The key theme in this chapter is integrating *collaboration*—forming powerful networks that can't be automated.

You don't have to reskill yourself *alone* in the automation age. What's unique about our time is that while millions of jobs will be automated, millions more will be seeded through social labor ecosystems, which take many forms.

In this chapter, I'll zero in on two of the "I"s in my Quad I matrix: innovation and improvisation. If there's any combination that reflects these two attributes best, it's entrepreneurship and invention. The two go hand in hand. You can't be an entrepreneur without the spirit of invention, that is, improvising something new to fit a specific purpose. Edison and Tesla needed to transport and sell electricity. IBM needed to store and process data. Apple wanted to put global communications in everyone's hands. None of those entrepreneurs and companies would've succeeded without innovation and improvisation.

Actually, let's get the sequence right: you can't innovate without *improvising*. Edison and his team didn't know which light bulb filament would work on the first few tries. Most of them burned up. He improvised by trying thousands of materials (and other inventors did, too). Entrepreneurship is thriving today, mostly because even in an age of corporate complacency, we still need bootstrappers who are trying new things.

While machines can try different combinations—based on algorithms and data—they are limited to what's in their programs. They won't pick something off the shop floor and see it if fits in a concept that may not work. They don't really "noodle" with things. They won't come up with thousands of drawings, like Leonardo did in his notebooks, in an attempt just to describe a natural process like water flowing.

AUTOMATION SNAPSHOT:
AWARD-WINNING ENTREPRENEURS

I visited and interviewed several entrepreneurs who, surprisingly, are *not* creating the latest smartphone messaging app or social media platform. They were innovating across a broad spectrum of commercial, industrial, and social applications. A handful of avatars in the evolving social ecosystem of innovators had won honors at the Chicago Innovation Awards, an annual event hosted by Tom Kuczmarski and Luke Tanen, the two executives behind the organization. They wanted to recognize a diverse mix of innovators from global corporate giants to social entrepreneurs. The event itself was dazzling, replete with live music, laser lights, an exciting video, and large performance stage. It was more like the Oscars than a staid business event. More than 1,000 attended to see the 20 winners among more than 500 nominees.[54] Here's a sampling of the awardees and why their innovations are important.

A Prick-Free Glucose Monitor. For diabetics, who have to constantly monitor their blood sugar levels, the most despised part of that process is pricking a finger to draw and test blood. It's uncomfortable for most—and it has to be done thousands of times. Abbott Labs' Freestyle Libre essentially automates the monitoring—with the finger prick. The device employs a wireless skin sensor (good for 14 days) that wirelessly transmits glucose readings to a remote device.[55]

Fresh Salads—In Vending Machine. This delivery system is hardly known for freshness. The junk food that usually resides within these machines may have been sitting there for months. Farmer's Fridge developed a way to stock vending machines with fresh salads. The food is not only good for you, it's palatable. Their motto: "Eat Happier."[56]

Reducing Document Review Time. If you're on a legal team, you often need to review thousands of documents. Equify employs AI and real-time analytics to cut review time by up to 40 percent.[57]

History and Memory Preserved in 3D. Holocaust survivors were recorded by the Illinois Holocaust Museum for all time in their Take a Stand Center. Not only were they captured in three-dimensional holograms, their images are tied into a natural-language AI interface that allows them to "answer" questions from the audience. When I saw this exhibit, it was life-altering.[58] (See my Afterword for more on this.)

ENTREPRENEURS AS IMPROVISERS

When I was researching this book, I interviewed several entrepreneurs who were embedded in communities that were ecosystems of people dedicated to starting and growing companies. How do I define ecosystem? In nature, it's a system of relationships. Bees, for example, need pollen. In the process of gathering it and making their own food (honey), they fertilize plants, which can then produce seeds, reproduce themselves, and ultimately feed us. On a human scale, the social/commercial ecosystem includes:

- **Idea Generators.** These are the folks who come up with the seeds of businesses. What service or product will the enterprise produce? Who will be their customers? How will it serve a need? Raw ideas are where everything starts.

- **Social Entrepreneurs.** They are addressing a social problem. How do we get more homeless people into shelters? How can we address food shortages in urban "deserts"? How do we reduce gang violence and crime?

- **Better Mousetrap Makers.** How do we make an everyday object, tool, or application better? Can you make a better spatula? Can you design more age-friendly appliances and phones?

- **Financiers.** Getting a company up and running takes money. "Angel" investors, venture capitalists, and other investors are always needed to get the money to get something going.

- **Marketers and Communicators.** You can have the greatest idea in the world, but if you can't sell or communicate its value to the world, then you're not going to stay in business very long. Messaging, public relations, and marketing help entrepreneurs tell their stories.

- **Techies.** Even with AI increasingly entering this space, you'll still need coders, data analysts and all kinds of tech support. Someone has to write and fix code.

- **Customer Support.** Although a lot of customer service is handled by robo interfaces, for complicated questions, you still need someone on the phone to walk you through something. The human touch is essential.

These are the basic roles in a social ecosystem. There are many more, of course. As you can see, though, it's more than just about innovation. Every person in this system needs to improvise and integrate in some way. The starchy idea that someone has to "stay in their lane" or stay "siloed" is obsolete in the age of automation.

You need to be able to move in and out of different roles, much like a sailor on a small ship. Navigation is essential, but you still need to be able to unfurl and trim the sails, avoid storms, and fix things as they break (as best you can). Although certainly most of us become specialists in life, it's the ability to take on different attributes that will count the most. You'll have to work with others to do so. Collaboration makes you part of the ecosystem.

WHY *QUAD I'S* ARE IDEAL IN SOCIAL LABOR ECOSYSTEMS

Anyone who's ever been in a meeting with creative people knows how things can go off the rails. Ideas are flying left and right. There doesn't seem to be any direction. Although it seems chaotic, this is the environment in which Quad I's thrive, so let's revisit what they do:

1. **Innovation.** They break things, tear things down, and see what's been done. Then they try something new. It's this willingness to go beyond the pale that will transcend any kind of machine learning. Maybe what they want to know isn't in the data, but it's out there to be discovered.

2. **Integration.** They work with the best tools and systems they have. They work well with others to collaborate. They learn how to integrate their ideas and products into an existing system.

3. **Insight.** They're not just looking into or at data or patterns, they are interpreting and looking beyond their spreadsheets. They are asking questions on what's behind the story they are seeing. They are creating a narrative. What is the story? What does it mean?

4. **Improvisation.** They are using the narrative to tell the story to others. If it doesn't work, they change the story when the facts change. They are not afraid to fail. They do it in front of others and are learning from failure and collaborating in doing so.

HOW INCUBATORS AND ACCELERATORS BOOST THE SOCIAL LABOR ECOSYSTEM

Sometimes you need a little help to become a Quad I. No one possesses all the skills they need. It's not out of the question to ask for some help. I discovered that there are hundreds of incubators and accelerators that help those with business and social venture ideas.

An *incubator* is pretty much like the warm place where eggs are hatched, only it's for entrepreneurs. Incubators are all over the world, sometimes sponsored by universities, but also by private companies like TechStars. They nurture companies into viable enterprises by providing support with marketing, coding, and a whole range of services.

An *accelerator* is the next rung of the social ecosystem. Also sponsored by universities and private firms, accelerators take going concerns and take them to the next level: say a company is selling $1 million annually in something and wants to sell $10 million annually. Accelerators provide the fuel through experienced professionals and investors.

Katlin Smith had an idea based on a need: how to create healthy baking mixes and baked goods. There weren't many of these products on the market, and they were mostly absent from supermarket shelves. As a student at the University of Chicago's Booth School of Business, she entered Booth's New Venture Challenge accelerator program with the idea of growing her idea into a thriving business. Competing against 100 other teams, she eventually won $30,000 to seed her enterprise Simple Mills.[59] Her original idea was spurred by the idea that clean eating could help alleviate chronic joint pain.

With a mission of enriching lives through "simple, delicious, real foods," Simple Mills not only strives to offer healthy alternatives to sugar- and salt-laden products, but offers "food that tastes great in the moment and nourishes your body for the long term."[60] She eventually raised more than $5 million; now her products are in more than 1,700 stores. What she gained from Booth's program is a pastiche of support, capital, and experience, which is what ecosystems provide. Very little of this process involves smooth sailing, though. Her path was littered with rejections.

"I never thought about how big I could get," she told me, instead focusing on getting her idea to market and building a business around it.[61]

DIGITAL TRANSFORMATION

The merger of AI, data, machines, analytics, and robotics is what industry observers call a "digital transformation." Entire industries are being rebuilt around this concept. How do companies find new customers? They pool and analyze data and use predictive analytics to make educated guesses on how to identify and attract people to buy their products and services.

Digital transformation is about reworking an old model into a new delivery system. Let's take bookstores. I love them, especially the experience of

AUTOMATION SNAPSHOT: FINTECH FINDS NEW CUSTOMERS

What happens when you manage to integrate your ideas into a business plan? You find new ways to help people or sell new products and services. Then you discover hybrid approaches to combine machine learning and analytics with hands-on people skills.

One industry subset that exemplifies this merger of machines and minds is *fintech*, the industry behind personal financial services technology. Fintech is bringing everything from money management to tax planning to the average person. Most know fintech through some of the most popular applications such as PayPal. Yet fintech goes far beyond money transfers into the realm of money management, financial planning, and even saving for retirement.

Fintech is growing by leaps and bounds because most people hate dealing with money issues. Few of us are ever taught how to create a risk-adjusted, managed portfolio, yet we are told to do just that in our 401(k) plans. Enter fintech, which seeks to automate most of that gnarly process.

Personal Capital is one fintech tool that allows users to analyze their net worth, link accounts, and make money decisions. The beauty of this tool—and other robo advisers—is that you don't need to step into a bank or brokerage firm to utilize this Swiss Army knife of money management. You can do nearly everything on your phone, tablet, or home computer. Want to see your credit card or 401(k) balance? Want to know how to save more money and cut expenses? How about setting up a retirement plan? Most of these often difficult tasks are automated. Robo advisers are providing services to millions who need to deal with money but want to do it in a seamless, emotionally safe way.[62]

But services like Personal Capital aren't the whole solution. Not everything can be explained in a digital application, especially if it involves something as personal and complex as money and tax management. People still need to be part of the ecosystem. According to State Street Corporation, which manages more than $2.5 trillion, nearly "64% of retail investors say they will want *personalized* advice in the near future, while 62% expect do-it-yourself capability such as tools that enable them to self-manage their investments."[63]

As you get older, money issues become ever more complex. You need to do estate planning and help parents. You may need to save for college and retirement—at the same time (see the appendix). Then there are nasty blips like unemployment and health issues. Technology won't come to the rescue. You'll definitely have to improvise, but integrating and automating your money life is an incredibly helpful start.

---

browsing and discovering a new subject or author. But they've largely been automated by Amazon, and it's mostly humbled or vanquished competitors. You have to physically walk to a bookshelf in the old model. Maybe you find something, maybe you don't, but no bookstore can have every book in print on display. Yet data intelligence and integration can help you find books that suit your interests. Log in, do a search. Algorithms will pop up suggested titles. You didn't have to think about it or go into a bookstore.

What's happened? The route between you and the books you want just got shorter. It took seconds and you didn't have to leave your computer or phone screen. And you have access to millions of books. Does this dehumanize the experience of reading or finding books? In a way, yes. It's also put independent booksellers and even larger chains out of business (e.g., Borders), but made local booksellers much more savvy. My local bookstore—This Old Book in Grayslake—has focused on selling collectible books and publications online. Its clientele is growing. So the digital transformation works both ways. Again, improvisation, the soul of innovation, is necessary to survive, but it will have to happen neighborhood by neighborhood in many places. Entire communities will need to be transformed as well along the lines of healthy social/commercial ecosystems.

WHY COMMUNITIES WILL NEED TO BE REINVENTED

The social/commercial ecosystem sometimes involves complete overhauls of communities if they are to survive in the automation age. South Chicago, which I explored in the first chapter, is hollowed out but struggling to reinvent itself. Once teeming with workers and their families with decent paychecks from local mills, it's fighting a battle with unemployment, gangs, and social decay. The once-proud industrial cathedral of the community—U.S. Steel's South Works—is a massive vacant lot along Lake Michigan, awaiting a mega-developer who never seems to materialize with the right plan or the hundreds of millions of dollars needed to redevelop a piece of real estate that's both a toxic waste site and sheer acreage that rivals the downtown Chicago Loop. A temporary-looking park memorializing the plant and its workers gazes north toward the magnificent and distant Chicago skyline.

If we're to embrace innovation, improvisation, and integration in the thinking machine age, we need to rebuild communities around these human traits. South Chicago was trying to do that with a new business incubator. Where once an integrated steel mill loomed over Lake Michigan, the community is attempting to reinvent itself. The insight here is that unlike steelmaking, which integrates a *system* from limestone and coal mining to the hot rolling/finishing/storage/delivery of steel, these communities need to be integrated directly with people. Places like South Chicago will need the kind of leadership that knows how to rebuild. Educated and experienced people will need to be part of the revival. A whole network of new people need to get involved and do some hard work. South Chicago won't become Silicon Valley. There's much more that needs to take place.

The ecosystem is at the heart of this process, yet we can't isolate one factor and over-concentrate on it. There's much more at play that we can't ignore.

WHY INNOVATION ISN'T ENOUGH: WE'LL HAVE TO COLLABORATE

It's easy to be smitten with the idea of innovation. Our best and brightest business heroes have this innovation halo. Steve Jobs is a saint to many. Apple's products, in their heyday, were products of cultlike devotion (I'm not so sure if that's true today). Elon Musk, the founder of SpaceX and Tesla Motors, also wore a similar crown, although it's been much tarnished. He is said to be the model for the modern Tony Stark, the industrialist who's also Iron Man.

Yet there's a peril in worshipping innovation alone. There's so much more to thriving in the automation age that a single factor isn't enough. It never had been. Another reason that we'll have to work together in ecosystems is that there may not be enough workers to go around to fill every position. Pure demographics will rule the shrinking labor force. That means more AI and robots—and we'll have to work with them.

Modern industrial societies are mostly getting older, not younger. And as women move up the economic ladder everywhere—particularly in the developing world—they have fewer children. Both are long-term trends that translate into fewer future workers. Fortunately, the workforce is becoming more diverse.

Observes Ruchir Sharma, chief global strategist at Morgan Stanley Investment Management, "for much of the world, robots will stand alongside immigrants, women and the elderly as the fourth pool of labor."[64]

Yes, we'll most likely work *with* robots in many new jobs. Integration will be the linchpin of those relationships. Sharma continues:

> Whether by design or accident, many of the countries with the most rapidly aging populations already have the most robots. According to the International Federation of Robotics, the nations with the highest density of industrial robots include South Korea, Japan and Germany. The United States ranked eighth. China is well behind, but on the bright side—arguably—it had the world's fastest-growing robot population.[65]

The graying of world populations is inevitable. Since Sharma wrote this piece in 2016, more research has emerged that shows how, given the reduction of working-age populations, future workers will collaborate with robots. There just may not be enough workers to perform what needs to be done. According to a report by McKinsey, the aging U.S. workforce alone will mean that by 2060, the over-65 cohort of the population will reach 98 million or nearly a quarter of the entire population. As it stands now, some 10,000 Americans are turning 65 every day.[66]

You also need to factor in that many countries are restricting immigration for political reasons. Japan and Korea have never really been receptive to immigration. Europe is deeply conflicted over mass migration. And the United States is also struggling with the issue.

Restricting immigration has its downside. Many jobs that *could* go to younger workers *willing* to be trained could be sitting unfilled, an anecdote I heard frequently while researching this book. It raises the possibility that older workers who need to be reskilled simply don't want to take that leap. That's another issue entirely, and one that's difficult to illuminate. Hardly anyone will tell a survey that they're *unwilling* to learn something new. It may be that like most people, they are resistant to new knowledge. That invites the question, though: if more workers feel they are too old, have left the workforce, are unable to embrace new skills, or simply don't want to work, will that create an opening for even more automation?

If this is true to any extent, that means that more, not fewer, workers will be collaborating with robots. Notes MIT Economist David Autor: "journalists and expert commentators tend to overstate the extent of machine substitution for human labor and ignore the strong complementarities between automation and labor that increase productivity, raise earnings and augment demand for labor."[67]

Maybe this is too optimistic a view, but the demographic and potential labor shortage numbers are powerful indicators of the workforce in the future. Those who wish to keep working, in addition to embracing my Quad I matrix, will certainly have to adopt Autor's "complementarities" to work with machines.

FINAL NOTES

What does it take to become a Quad I? As you've seen, it's a continual challenge, like climbing a mountain. Being part of a social ecosystem helps, of course. If you can find a community of entrepreneurs or join an incubator or accelerator program, you'll find support. Collaboration, for many, is the most powerful social activity that will aid your success.

The one insight that's all-important is that you don't need to do any of this alone. Reinvention takes planning. You need to talk to people, explore local college programs, and talk to others who've started and run new ventures. Incubators and accelerators are important parts of the ecosystem, but you can also find support through local community colleges and job centers. There are also thousands of books on the subject.

You'll also need to reach within yourself, which is the opposite of seeking social support. Tapping your own creativity is a key part of this process, which is what I'll explore in the next chapter.

SIX

The New Synergistic Creativity: How Multidisciplinary Invention Will Take Center Stage

In addition to collaboration, personal creativity will be more important than ever. This chapter explores the synergies that enable individuals to make things with smart machines—and why that's important.

Prof. Rob Twardock is giving me a tour of a machine-happy room at the College of Lake County (CLC), the community college that's just up the street from me. Rob, a friend and neighbor, is department chair of the Engineering Transfer Department at CLC. Trained as a civil engineer at the University of Illinois-Champaign Urbana, he worked as a practicing engineer before launching his teaching career.[8]

Inside what is known as the Baxter Innovation Lab (a work space funded by the drug company Baxter in Deerfield, Illinois) are an array of tools and computers. Some are standard for a fabrication, or "fab" lab, but many are smart machines that require a computer input and some knowledge of coding. There are also manual machines such as lathes and sanders than don't require computer instruction. Algorithms embedded in specialized software are the brains that drive most of the newer machines, which include 3D printers, laser cutters and CNC mills, and routers. The idea behind the fab lab, part of an international network of similar spaces, is to encourage college students to walk in and make something. These are high-end *maker spaces*, little creative islands that have sprouted up in varying locales from local libraries to universities. (I toured about a dozen such spaces during my research).

"We encourage people to make things and even screw up," Twardock told me.[69] "Students learn as much from their mistakes as their successful designs."

What is special about maker spaces is that they encourage and enable synergistic creativity. You need to be able to work with computer-driven tools to make things from scratch.

"They've brought the ability to make prototypes and proof of concept models to the masses as a results of inexpensive desktop digital fabrication, "Twardock adds. "Prototypes or one-off designs that used to cost thousands of dollars and take weeks to produce can now be made in minutes or hours for a fraction of the cost."

For example, let's say you wanted to make an entire chess set. You could easily find an open-source (free) 3D model on the Internet and download it into a computer hooked up to a 3D printer. Once you set up your project—and tweaked it a bit—you'd program the printer to go to work. Based on the computer instructions from the program, the printer would melt plastic resin to create the chess pieces. Voila! After several hours of production, you'd have a freshly made chess set, among thousands of other things made from scratch.

MAKING STARTS IN CHILDHOOD

Seeing the CLC Innovation Lab brought me back to my dad's basement workshop. In my child's eye, I once again saw all of the tools he had amassed from a hulking bandsaw to dozens of screwdrivers, hammers, saws, chisels, and various electronic parts. For larger projects, he had a table saw, grinders, and drill press. And so many parts! Screws, washers, old speakers, and ancient Dictaphones, which even into the 1960s used Edison's wax cylinder technology to record memos. My dad's workshop was a veritable museum of old components and fasteners that, in his depression-era sensibility, could be invaluable in future projects.

I tinkered a lot as a boy, building crystal radios and amplifiers from kits and playing around with sundry motors and a chemistry set. I even had my own "lab" under the stairs next to the workshop, where I pretended I was an astronaut doing a space walk. My orbital adventures came to a violent halt when I fell back and hit a piece of marble. I think I cracked it in half—with my head. Nevertheless, my role in my dad's domain was to identify and know where every single tool and fastener was stored. I had to know where to look when he asked me to find a tool for one of his major projects from fixing his cars to building an addition to our tiny Cape Cod, bursting at the seams with four boys and two adults. Oddly enough, knowing the names of tools did wonders for my memory.

I can still recall the name of each tool and what it did, using them many times myself. It was our own maker space before computers in my mode of unvarnished innocence. At a time when the streets of America were on fire, Vietnam was raging, and our greatest leaders were being gunned down, I was learning the basics of synergistic creativity in my own way, which is how many of us should embrace our own fabrication dreams. Fifty years into the future, I still tinker with the tools and skills I learned in my dad's workshop, even recently rebuilding and reengineering one of my electric violins. You don't need sophisticated tools to become a maker. Like a lot of kids, I started out with Lincoln logs, Play-Doh, Legos (which can become robots now), Erector Sets, and endless piles of spare parts. It doesn't take much to get going, but creativity is the key. Just start goofing around with things that others consider to be junk. Start rummaging around and building something.

WHAT YOU CAN DO IN A MAKER SPACE

While it's useful to have some academic grounding in basic use of machine tools, coding, math, engineering, and design, a personal passion to create something can be a source of motivation to build something.

"We have students use the lab as part of their engineering coursework, but also encourage them to work on personal projects, which is where we see the creativity really blossom," Twardock found. When I asked Rob what attributes the maker of today should possess, he gave me a short list:

1) **An Analytic Mind That Is Engaged in Problem Solving.** The solution is rarely right in front of you, so you'll need to experiment—and fail—a lot.

2) **You'll Need a Math Background or the Ability to Do It.** Those formulas and equations will come in handy, especially in programming machines, designing, and fabricating parts. Being good at math also correlates back to #1—excelling at analytic problem solving.

3) **The Ability and Love to Make Things, to Tinker and Take Existing Products Apart.** Although there are hundreds of kits that give you

all of the parts—some assembly required—you often have to improvise. What if you get the wrong part or something doesn't fit right?

4) **You'll Need Some Coding.** Sure, eventually computers will be able to
program themselves, but knowing some software language really helps.

5) **Being a Maker.** This is the merger of machines and computers. You
have to know how things connect to each other and how to operate
computer-driven machines. Being well rounded in manual machining,
shop tools, coding, and digital fabrication makes a good maker.

6) **Troubleshooting Is Critical.** Things rarely go right the first time
around. What went wrong? How can you fix it? Here's where improvisation comes in again.

7) **Thrive on the Process and Making It Cool.** You have to be comfortable with knowing that there may not be instant gratification or not
immediately knowing the answer. It's often a journey without a clear
road map.

Most importantly, fab labs and maker spaces bridge the gap between the
growing labor needs of the automation age and the skills needed to adapt
to the growing merger between AI, smart machines, and manufacturing.
Shop floors today (and in the future) in advanced digital manufacturing will
need specialized workers who understand not only how these tools operate
but how they can be fixed and programmed to do even more demanding
tasks. Modern workplaces demand workers who know math, coding, basic
mechanical knowledge, visualization, and some degree of creativity. It's
these synergies that will add value to their labor. They will be building
things more with their minds and less with their bodies.

A SAMPLING OF WHAT YOU'D NEED IN
EDUCATIONAL SUPPORT

Building up a synergistic creativity tool kit involves more than just walking into a maker space and tinkering around with 3D printers. Education is
important to know how to make things with smart machines.

A program that engages you in the new realities of the automation age
requires that you know something about robotics, mechanical systems, and
automation on several different levels. What do you need to know about
electronics, computers, and even old-fashioned pneumatic systems? You can
learn these things in a modern four-year engineering program, which of

course also requires several math and science courses, or enter into certificate or associate-degree programs on the community college level. One important thing to note: all of these programs require that you take and understand math and have the ability to code.

Even at the community college level, the amount of knowledge you can obtain is substantial. You can apply it anywhere in the advanced/digital manufacturing workplace. For example, CLC's mechatronics program offers a sequence that teaches automation principles, robotic design/construction, mechanical systems, pneumatics/hydraulics, and systems integration.[70] While you may not know what all of these subjects entail, taken as a whole, this kind of program will give you a workable overview of how smart machines work in the modern manufacturing floor.

More importantly, knowledge in a mechatronics programs—integrating a number of technologies—will give you all-important skills so that you can design, install, program, and integrate smart machines. These skills will be far more useful and portable. What kinds of jobs do these translate to? Here's a sampling:

- Technicians in automation, robotics, electromechanical, and mechatronics systems
- Programmable Logic Controller Technicians/Installers. You will be able to program the brains of smart machines.
- Maintenance Technicians. Workers will be needed to fix and maintain robots.
- Robot Operators, Installers, and Technicians
- Mechanical Engineering Technicians
- Technical Sales Representatives

In short, even though most approaching this field may not know exactly what these roles are—and job titles and descriptions are changing—think *integration*. Manufacturing is not going away, but anyone interested in making things for a living will need this enhanced digital skill set. Even people selling the machines themselves will need some understanding of how integration works. Will some of these jobs eventually be automated as machines learn how to fix and program themselves? That's always a possibility, although those autonomous machine skills may be years away.

Engineers of all kinds, even engineering technicians, will be in demand as shop floors and factories increasingly automate. Although it would be desirable for society to produce more enlightened licensed engineers, it's generally difficult for most students to get into four-year college engineering programs. They are selective and you need above-average test scores in the math and sciences sections on the ACT and SAT.

One bright spot about technical education offerings: they are widely available. Most counties and cities have fairly well-funded community or city colleges, which are increasingly offering these kinds of programs. Their tuition rates are usually much less than a four-year school, and there's no room and board (they are commuter colleges).

Even high schools are getting on board, upgrading what used to be known as "shop" or "vocational" classes. Now computers are finding their way into modern high school technical curricula with an emphasis on design and preengineering skills.

HOW MAKING SOMETHING LOCALLY IS SYNERGISTIC

When I was examining the maker space/fab lab movement, I found synergistic creativity blossoming, sometimes in unexpected places. I had been speaking at libraries in my area on my Tesla book *Lightning Strikes* and discovered that most of them had maker spaces, many of them brand new. Like the CLC Innovation Lab, they had laser cutters and 3D printers, only on a much smaller scale. They also had sewing machines, pattern cutters, and other basic tools.

In my local library, the library foundation had funded our own maker space. They called their area, which was formerly study rooms, "The Hub." Since this was a new community resource designed to engage patrons at all levels, there was a generous amount of support. Specialized librarians are available to advise and assist anyone with a 3D printer, cutting/engraving tools, sewing machines, and even audio/visual production equipment. There were even maker kits that could be checked out. You could make tiny robots or basic video games. The space was also supported by ongoing programming.

Why are maker spaces being added to traditional community institutions like libraries? They are on the vanguard of reconnecting people to the art of making things, which has been lost in an endless vortex of consumption, social media, and countless other distractions. In the larger sense, the maker movement is rewiring brains to the creative side of cognition, something invaluable in the automation age.

Maker spaces are part of something much bigger, though. They are an outgrowth of the maker movement, which was seeded by Maker Media and

AUTOMATION SNAPSHOT: THE FAB LAB/MAKER
SPACE/MAKER FAIRE MOVEMENT

If you just want to dip you toes in the water of smart machines or bump up your game, it would be wise to explore a fab lab, maker space, or larger event such as a maker or mini-maker faire, which are being held all over the world.

Fab labs are much more than maker spaces on steroids. They are a support network that grew out of research and a "fab charter" at the Massachusetts Institute of Technology (MIT) and Professor Mitchell Resnick. The mission of the fab labs is straightforward: "to support digital and personal fabrication in academics, business and community outreach in the spirit of MIT."[71]

By making things using the synergistic creativity of software, smart tools, and our own hands, we're transforming ideas into solid objects. It's something our species has done from the first hominids crafting a tool out of a stick to our current automation age. There's more, because it involves building experience in a number of ways and literally creating new circuits to do new things. Here are the core values of the US Fab Lab Network:[72]

- **Experimentation:** We believe experimentation is the key to invention and overall economic sustainability for the U.S.
- **Hands-on Learning:** We strongly value and support hands-on learning.
- **Open Access:** People of all ages and backgrounds should have open access to space, equipment, and technology among people of all ages and backgrounds.
- **Collaboration:** We believe collectively we can do more than anyone can accomplish alone.
- **Problem Solving:** We believe all people can help solve real world problems.
- **Empowerment:** We strive to empower businesses, entrepreneurs, inventors, and the general public.
- **Creativity:** We believe that all people have creative talent.
- **Achievement:** We believe Science, Technology, Engineering, and Math (STEM) education can be fun and attainable for all, not just engineers and scientists.

Note the egalitarian ethos of the fab labbers. It's a ground-up, open-access process. No longer is fabrication the exclusive domain of male engineers, scientists, and designers. Anyone can make anything, and they should have the access to tools to do so. They are not elitists. The technology that can reshape our future belongs to—and should be used by—*everyone* who wants to give it a try. Their goals go even further in creating a "robust community" for a "new generation of entrepreneurs, inventors and artisans." They are training problem solvers, people who see something that they can tackle and add value.

MAKE magazine in 2005. Although claiming to be a grassroots movement, the commercial arm of the movement markets components like Arudino controllers, the brains of do-it-yourself robots.[73] With these devices—sold in kits—you can make any number of electronic gadgets. You can even hack existing technology like cellphones.

The maker movement's showcases are two major "maker faires" in the San Francisco Bay and New York City areas, although there are more than 170 spin-off faires or "mini-faires" from Berlin to Shenzhen, featuring robotmakers, crafters, and electronic gizmos that amaze and delight. Even bookstores are now hosting mini-faires while offering the maker products.[74]

Who knows who will come out of a maker space with a sense that they can build something, tear it apart, and create an entirely new system? These are the seed nurseries of innovation. If you want to become a Quad I person, your journey may just begin at your local library or community college.

SOME DEEPER DEFINITIONS

What do I mean when we unite hands with minds and machines? Synergistic creativity is something that involves integration with other *systems.* Let's say you're doodling on a piece of paper. That's certainly creative. But to be *synergistic*, you need to take that doodle beyond its isolated page. Let's say the doodle becomes a new kitchen tool or a work of art. But you need to do more to bring it into the world. You may use computer-aided design (CAD) connected to a 3D printer to make it plastic. You're not only being creative, you're employing a synergy with software and hardware to bring your creation into the world. That's not to say that sculptors like Michelangelo working with blocks of marble or chapel ceilings weren't being synergistic. He had to know his materials and interact with them. In my definition, synergies go beyond one object. They involve algorithms, machines that make things, and even AI.

Of course, CAD and 3D printers are nothing new, although their synergies are creating a range of wonderful things from interactive artificial limbs to the tallest skyscrapers in the world. Each creation starts with an image or vision but needs a tremendous amount of computing power to make it take shape. They are now basic tools in personal and advanced digital manufacturing.

Another key piece of synergistic creativity is the ability to merge your ideas—and often your body—into machines and software. The best possible artificial limbs are linked to the users' brains, so that electrical impulses can move the limbs. This transformation is *chimeric*, that is, it melds people and machines. (In mythology, a chimera was an animal that was goat, lion, and dragon—and usually ill tempered.)

HOW DO WE PROMOTE SYNERGISTIC CREATIVITY?

Here are two ways to orient your mind: *think globally and create locally.* That is, take on a problem and figure out how you can solve it—or go small and address it piece by piece. Some global problems are gargantuan, such as climate change and resource depletion, while others are more digestible such as providing better medical records. It depends on how challenged you want to be. How you think (see next chapter) involves asking the question: are you a *systems* thinker—you see the earth and universe as a system that can be understood and adjusted. Others are tinkerers or inventors. That's okay, too. They'd be happy with a smartphone app that told them the best way to pay off their student loans. Looking for some big projects? Try these monster issues on for size:

Global Warming and Climate Change. Scientists are in a broad consensus that it's happening on a global scale. Polar ice is melting. Sea levels are rising. Droughts, floods, wildfires, hurricanes, tornadoes are getting worse. What to do about it? Reducing the output of carbon dioxide and methane is a massive challenge. Enter "geo-engineering," where scientists believe they can engineer a solution through technology. There are, of course, smaller pieces of this puzzle: creating cheap, fossil-free energy one building at a time or conserving water. There are myriad possible solutions.

Automating Transportation. All of the major vehicle and tech companies from Apple to Google want a piece of this game. But it requires quantum leaps in AI, programming, machine vision, materials, and factories that will make autonomous vehicles. And there are lots of necessary innovations needed along the way: cheaper, lighter, and more energy-hoarding batteries; precise navigation systems; "seeing" pedestrians and accident situations; self-correcting driving technology. The innovation list also encompasses entirely new manufacturing plants to make these vehicles from new semiconductor chips to power their brains to the robots that will build them. Many vehicles already have these technologies, but they need to be refined.

Big Cures. Again, there's a lot of diseases that need major advances in knowledge and treatments. Alzheimer's, cancer, Parkinson's and diabetes top the list. Scientists and doctors are already employing big data and supercomputers to try to figure out which proteins and genes they can work on to stop these diseases. More work, of course, needs to be done. The only commonality is that communities of researchers are working across their own specialties to find cures. That's synergistic creativity on a global scale, which involves big dollars and economic impact. "Think of a cure for Alzheimer's," writes Bill Gates, the founder of Microsoft and one of the richest philanthropists in the world. "The disease costs the U.S. $236 billion a year, mostly to Medicare and Medicaid. A cure would immediately alter the budget of every state in the country, not to mention millions of lives."[75]

Better Materials. This sounds dull, but what if you created a road material that lasted for a century and wasn't harmful to the environment? Or an easily recharged battery that didn't require lithium? Or a building material that insulated your home so that you didn't have to spend as much money heating and cooling it? These are but a handful of challenges facing materials scientists and engineers. There are hundreds of thousands of roads, bridges, tunnels, electrical, transit, and water systems that need to be fixed and upgraded. Many of them were first installed more than a century ago. Infrastructure, combined with climate change and public health, will occupy our social agenda for the foreseeable future.

Of course, this is a daunting list. Any one of these issues is enough to make you despair or want to turn on a cable show or watch cat videos. My larger point is that in the automation age, we have many more *tools* to address these problems, but we will need more knowledge workers who know how to best use them. Yet before we retrain or reskill them, they will need the ability to understand synergistic creativity. We're all able to create, invent, integrate, and improvise. We just need to build those skills.

FINAL NOTES

As you've seen, synergistic creativity takes many forms. It can be tinkering in a maker space—or simply in a workshop of your own. You can even buy kits online or in bookstores. The general idea is that you're building, stripping down, experimenting, and often failing.

This route to creativity also involves working with code and smart machines. Think mechatronics, the hybrid of computers and basic machine tools. Because this form of thinking and doing isn't really in any one text-book, you'll need to be adventurous to find what you need. You may find a 3D printer in a public library or computer-aided design software in your local high schools. In every case, though, you're integrating and improvising—and gaining insights—into how to work creatively with soft-ware and hardware to do your bidding.

In the next chapter, I'll take an even deeper dive into creativity, only look-ing at what the brain does to get us where we need to be—and how you can enhance those functions.

SEVEN

Essential Mind Skills: What Will You Need to Know and Do

There's more to understanding and prospering in the world of automation than working in groups and having synergistic creativity. You will need to develop a powerful set of mind skills. This chapter will profile the most important skills to nurture.

Prof. Robert Shiller is holding center stage in an auditorium with a legendary history. He's keynoting a Neubauer Collegium lecture at the University of Chicago's Oriental Institute. Although most probably don't make this connection, the original Indiana Jones (and his father) were based on two real-life University of Chicago archaeologists—James Henry Breasted and Robert Braidwood (the institute's auditorium is named after Breasted). Both men made monumental contributions to the study of ancient civilizations, although they weren't treasure hunters dodging boulders or mummy curses. As if you needed more atmosphere for imagining movie plots or the men who discovered priceless relics, the adjoining museum includes a 17-foot-tall statue of King Tut and thousands of other antiquities from the Near East such as the winged bull from the palace of Persian King Sargon.[76]

The stories behind the artifacts have been meticulously detailed over the years by scholars, who were asking some interesting questions: Why did Egyptians spend so much time and expense mummifying kings and cats? What made the Persian Empire so powerful? Why is Mesopotamian culture called the "cradle of civilization"? While we don't have the precise answers, we have various narratives or story lines. We need to look backward and make educated guesses about how ancient civilizations functioned; the sciences of archaeology and anthropology help us fill in the plot details.

Narratives are the academic province of Shiller, who won the Nobel Prize in Economics and teaches at Yale. His classic *Irrational Exuberance* attempted to explain the narratives behind financial bubbles. In his lecture, Shiller sees narrative as a key tool in illuminating what happened in history and what is happening to us now.[77] While our interpretations can be all over the board, the narrative can be all important.

> "The human species, everywhere you go, is engaged in conversation," Shiller says. "We are wired for it: the human brain is built around narratives. We call ourselves *Homo sapiens*, but that may be something of a misnomer—*sapiens* means wise. The evolutionary biologist Stephen Jay Gould said we should be called *Homo narrator.* Your mind is really built for narratives, and especially narratives about other humans."[78]

What's unique about human narratives is that we are hardwired to internalize stories about how the world works. That means we believe some stories and not others. Our brains are organized to make sense of the world in this way. Otherwise, the bombardment of sensory and intellectual information coming at us would turn us into blubbering mush.

Narratives can become *memes*, that is, viral pieces of information that replicate themselves in the minds of others. They could take the form of a negative comment posted on social media, an image, or a silly video. Shiller says that these viral ideas can often become embedded realities for millions, even though they may have no basis in fact or are historically wrong.

> Narratives are contagious: they spread from one person to another. Some narratives disappear quickly; others can last a long time. I think of a narrative as a gem, something that you heard somewhere, and you think, I'll remember that next time I'm in a conversation. I'll use that. I'll say it. I'll try to present it right because I want it to have the effect that it had on me. That is a narrative. Narrative can, in the parlance of the internet, go viral.[79]

What's viral in the age of automation? That robots will eventually take *every* job or that they will completely replace human creativity *and* labor. Much or some of this may be true, but there's almost no precedent in history that tells us exactly what will happen. We only know that it's possible and *likely*, yet to what degree is up for speculation. If the robot takeover is driven by fear—which often drives popular narratives—then that's understandable. No one wants to be in the position of having one of the jobs likely to be lost to automation and believe that *my* livelihood is going to be axed.

Yet it's this uniquely human mix of dread, optimism, greed, insight, and fantasy that underlies our narratives on automation. At some point you have to concede that the future is unpredictable in so many ways; it's irrational to go around worrying about things that may never happen. Still, we need to understand the creative impulse and the neuroscience behind it before we start coming up with grand theories. There are definitely human attributes that are so complex that robots may never supersede us. First, though, let's explore the range of possible robot cognition.

ROBOTS AND COGNITION

Here's a narrative that's a staple of Hollywood films: the robot that learns how to think and *feel* like a person. Inspired by Mary Shelley's *Franken-stein* and Fritz Lang's silent classic *Metropolis*, we've been enthralled for several centuries by the idea of creating artificial, sentient beings that are *just like us*. Can this ever be possible? Sure, if you're a consumer of science fiction or see movies like *Ex Machina*, in which a humanoid robot thinks and battles her way out of her prison-like servitude.[80] The truth is more nuanced, of course. Human cognition and emotions are not entirely understood. Even so, it would take an epic amount of processing power to duplicate higher orders of thinking.

A piece of the robot takeover narrative (see my postscript on page 151) is that once they find out how to think and feel, in addition to taking our jobs, they will discover they despise us and eradicate us. That's the "robot rebellion" story arc. But that idea is often fanciful, because to take action, robots would probably have to reason and emote on *why* they don't like us and why we need to be pushed out of the way for global domination. In any case, academic research is much more grounded in what's likely to happen based on the capabilities of AI and its subset, machine learning. In an often-cited paper entitled "When Will AI Exceed Human Performance," a team of researchers don't reach any concrete answers on that question, although they come up with some estimates, based on a survey of AI experts.[81] Here are some predicted milestones about when machines will be able to "outperform humans" at higher-order tasks:

- **Translating Languages (2024).** You can access Google Translate now, but it's an imperfect tool. Idioms and their application are notoriously difficult, especially colloquialisms. Try to explain to a computer what "jumping the shark" really means (hint: it's not about *Jaws*).

- **Writing High-School Essays (2026).** There are many writing tools available now, but it is perennially difficult to write in one's voice. Most high school teachers and college admissions officers can spot less-than-original work.

- **Driving a Truck (2027).** This is a big AI/big data/autonomous vehicle project, but may be further away than this prediction indicates. It takes a tremendous amount of processing power to navigate changing weather conditions and bad drivers.

- **Working in Retail (2031).** This isn't a reference to self-checkouts or automated logistics, it's about robots walking the floor to help you find something. We're seeing this to a limited degree in some of Amazon's automated stores, but we're talking actual robots who help you find that perfect mother's or father's day gift.

- **Writing a Best-selling Book (2049).** I'm not convinced this is that far off; many best sellers are highly formulaic. Still, can a computer create the next James Bond or Harry Potter?

- **Working as a Surgeon (2053).** There are robotic surgeries now, although they are guided directly by a human doctor. An autonomous surgeon is a tall order, although they could improve on bedside manner.[82]

No matter which narrative you accept, the growing power of thinking machines can't be denied. The technology that enables machines to crunch data, see patterns, and take action is improving constantly, so it's best to take the long view and view specific predictions—and the years in which they may occur—with a grain of salt. You can embrace a *meta-narrative* (big picture) that some tasks will surely be automated because it makes economic sense to do so, while others may take so much computing power that it may make better sense to let a human keep his/her job. As the AI expert study concludes:

Researchers believe there is a 50% chance of AI outperforming humans in all tasks in 45 years and of automating all human jobs in 120 years, with Asian respondents expecting these dates much sooner than North Americans. These results will inform discussion amongst researchers and policymakers about anticipating and managing trends in AI. . . . To adapt public policy, we need to better anticipate these advances."[83]

If anything, expert testimony on the future involves an unreliable narrator since we often have cloudy crystal balls. Technologists can often envision machine domination. Writers and Hollywood directors can take that several steps further. Dystopian realists may have an even darker take. Techno-optimists see a silver lining in liberating us from labor, much the way Keynes opined in the 1930s.

AUTOMATION SNAPSHOT: ROBOT REPORTERS

Remember in earlier chapters when I talked about automation in my industry (journalism)? Ironically, since I penned my column with Bloomberg News from 2001 to 2009, mainstream journalism has become one of the most automated industries on the planet.

So-called "robot reporters" now do everything from corporate earnings reports to covering local sports events. How can that be possible? Well, earnings reports are pretty much all the same. The numbers (sales, profits, etc.) have to be reported in an identical format. This formula, of course, can be easily repeated by machines and then sent out in a press release. It's the journalistic equivalent to a machine assembling the same parts millions of times to make something uniform. The Associated Press, notes the *New York Times*, has gone from producing 300 automated earnings reports per quarter to more than 3,700.[84] Of course, as any business reporter will tell you (I can surely attest to this), writing an earnings summary is really tedious, so many of us don't mind ceding this task to machines.

Still, there's a loss of labor that's contributing to the downsizing of our profession. Nearly every major global news operation is using robot reporting in some form. Bloomberg News uses as system called "Cyborg" for one-third of its content. Hedge funds have even more sophisticated systems that grab, analyze, and trade on earnings news in seconds. Is there still room for real reporters in the automation age? Of course, and that's where the narrative comes in. We still need to identify the underlying story and tell readers what it means. *Meaning* is what makes a story come alive.

"The work of journalism is creative, it's about curiosity, it's about storytelling, it's about digging and holding governments accountable, it's critical thinking, it's judgment—and *that* is where we want our journalists spending their energy," Lisa Gibbs, a friend and the director of news partnerships for the AP, told the *New York Times*.[85]

Those who are already employed in the above professions (and others cited earlier), however, want to believe that their experience and ability to improvise *can't* be completely automated. Surgeons who can successfully navigate complications or a patient going into cardiac arrest are invaluable. Truck drivers have the ability to drive in all sorts of weather and deal with dangerous road conditions on the fly. This is even more critical for pilots: remember the pilot (Chesley Sullenberger) who landed his airliner in the Hudson River after both of his engines went out and saved everyone on board?[86]

The narrative that will occupy our minds is that we are threatened as workers, an endangered species because AI is getting so pervasive and capable of doing cognitive work. Before we push this argument further, though, let's examine what humans do when they think and create. It's an important stepping-off point in understanding the automated workplace.

HOW PEOPLE REALLY THINK

Storytelling is a human capability that may elude machines in the broader sense. Only we can answer questions like "why was Odysseus cursed," or "what is Harry Potter really about," or "why is the film *Blade Runner* still one of the best science fiction films?" Of course, there's more to the story than our narrative sense of self, place, and time. We respond to the narrative of the outside world with *all* of our senses. Our bodies and minds are synergistic— working together—to respond, adapt, create, and survive. If I were to "reverse engineer" how this process works, I would start with three things that humans do pretty well, which are often presented by academics as "bottlenecks to computerization." This is from the Oxford study (Frey and Osborne):[87]

Creative Intelligence. This is pure synergy, where we interact with materials, the environment, and our own ideas to create something new and original. Although the Oxford researchers only chose two categories, it extends to all fields to knowledge from algebra to zoology. This is the core of my Quad I rubric. Its foundation is:

1) Originality. The ability to come up with unusual or clever ideas about a given topic or situation, or to develop creative ways to solve a problem.

2) Fine Arts. Knowledge of theory and techniques required to compose, produce, and perform works of music, dance, visual arts, drama, and sculpture.

Social Intelligence. Under the general umbrella of "emotional intelligence," this group combines our sense of the other and how we can work with people, or at least have some idea of how to interact with them. This translates into collaboration and integration—if we do it right. People in health care and most social services know this "human touch" realm well. And it's incredibly difficult to automate. It consists of:

1) Social Perceptiveness. Being aware of others' reactions and understanding why they react as they do.

2) Negotiation. Bringing others together and trying to reconcile differences.

3) Persuasion. Persuading others to change their minds or behavior.

4) Assisting and Caring for Others. Providing personal assistance, medical attention, emotional support, or other personal care to others such as coworkers, customers, or patients.

Perception and Manipulation. This is the mind-body link, which encompasses everything from playing cards to playing the violin. What we do with our hands and feet is an interplay of complex neuronal signals, intention, and muscle memory, and allows us to do a variety of things from putting a spin on a tennis ball to sewing intricate patterns. It involves:

1) Finger Dexterity. The ability to make precisely coordinated movements of the fingers of one or both hands to grasp, manipulate, or assemble very small objects.

2) Manual Dexterity. The ability to quickly move your hand, your hand together with your arm, or your two hands to grasp, manipulate, or assemble objects.

3) Cramped Work Space, Awkward Positions. How often does a job require working in cramped work spaces that require getting into awkward positions? While robots are probably best suited for cleaning sewers, disabling bombs, and exploring hostile planets, you will still need plumbers getting under sinks, mechanics pulling out parts, and artists lying on their backs to paint frescoes on ceilings.[88]

HOW THIS ALL FITS TOGETHER IN THE AGE OF AUTOMATION

The sum of the parts equals the whole. Emotions, logic, hand/body skills, and so many other human attributes make up who we are. How does this translate into an ideal Quad I person? First, one should be able to work *on,* *beside,* and *with* machines. Second, we will need to integrate what we know with what we can do. Evolution is essential. Then we will need to adapt. We will need to do the following:

Focus on Higher-Order Skills. This is the integration of emotion, reasoning, and machine knowledge. "Social, emotional and higher cognitive skills, such as creativity, critical thinking and complex information processing will also see growing demand," write James Manyika and Kevin Sneader of the McKinsey Global Institute.[89] They estimate that from 400 million to 800 million workers will be displaced by automation by 2030, depending on how quickly industry adopts AI and its associated technologies.[90] What will blunt the impact of automation is a combination of better training, investment in human capital, and redesigning the workplace to better integrate with machines.

Relational Reasoning. As we've seen earlier, machines are competent at seeing patterns in data, but how good are they at connecting big dots? Some relationships are hardwired in our brains—e.g., "tiger or hissing snake equals danger"—while others are irrational—"that smell reminds me of Paris." Our neurons have billions of connections with thoughts, memories, sounds, smells, equations, and experiences. That's a ton of network processing. According to the American Association for the Advancement of Science:

> Humans are generally pretty good at relational reasoning, a kind of thinking that uses logic to connect and compare places, sequences, and other entities. But the two main types of AI— statistical and symbolic—have been slow to develop similar capacities. Statistical AI, or machine learning, is great at pattern recognition, but not at using logic. And symbolic AI can reason about relationships using predetermined rules, but it's not great at learning on the fly.[91]

Another way to understand relational reasoning is to think like a jazz musician. The best players know the keys and meters that are the foundation of what they're doing. They know the ground rules, but then they improvise based on those rules—sometimes throwing them out entirely. Will a machine create a Charlie Parker solo? Or improvise a comedy routine on the fly?

Critical Thinking. Sure, machines can organize and analyze tons of data, but can they make aesthetic, moral, or ethical judgments? Can they come up with a new philosophy of mind, spirit, or politics? In the machine age, being Quad I smart means being a competent critical thinker.

The "New Smart" combines book learning, on-the-fly improvisation, and a willingness to throw out blueprints. You have to be able to look at what's been done in the past and say "let's try this again, only in a different way." Failure is a viable option, because that's how we learn. We have to be humble. As Ed Hess, a business professor and author of *The New Smart: Rethinking Human Excellence in the Smart Machine Age*, notes:[92]

- The New Smart will be determined not by what or how you know but by the quality of your thinking, listening, relating, collaborating, and learning.
- Quantity is replaced by quality. And that shift will enable us to focus on the hard work of taking our cognitive and emotional skills to a much higher level.
- We will spend more time training to be open-minded and learning to update our beliefs in response to new data.
- We will practice adjusting after our mistakes, and we will invest more in the skills traditionally associated with emotional intelligence.
- The New Smart will be about trying to overcome the two big inhibitors of critical thinking and team collaboration: our ego and our fears. Doing so will make it easier to perceive reality as it is, rather than as we wish it to be. In short, we will embrace humility. That is how we humans will add value in a world of smart technology.

Ah yes, humility. There's a lot we don't know and we're loath to admit it. We put on blinders when it comes to the dark trends in our lives, our worldview, and our work life. Surely, *my* job won't be automated. *My* skills are essential. Take it from someone who's been laid off a number of times for any number of reasons (none of them really due to automation): it's hard to be open-minded when it comes to one's own livelihood. The most difficult thing is to accept a pessimistic view when it comes to what we are doing.

That's where *emotional intelligence* comes in. As Prof. Shiller explained at the beginning of the chapter, we tend to lock into a narrative. In this case, for millions, it's that robots will *never* replace our work. Why do we cling to this idea? Behavioral economists like Shiller have found that we tend to rate ourselves more highly than others (e.g., we are better drivers, smarter, etc.). We also tend to "frame" situations that cause us less emotional pain. It's hard to let go of something once it's in our possession (like a job, object, or profession). And we feel *maximum* emotional pain in losing, so we avoid it at all costs. We grasp at unrealistic ideas because it's part of our self-narrative.

On a larger scale, narratives often manipulate markets with disastrous results. Take the housing/credit/stock bust of 2007–2009. Nobody wanted to believe that home prices would ever decline: these were people's homes, after all! But emotional anchors to "home sweet home" led to a massive global bubble bursting, irrational themes that we couldn't detach from reality, or "real determinants of market moves," Shiller remarks in his classic *Irrational Exuberance.* "Many of those determinants are in our minds. They are the 'animal spirits' that John Maynard Keynes thought drove the economy."[93]

Back to Keynes again. The economist realized that he couldn't explain what was going on in the stock market by math alone. Something else had to be in play, so he came up with the phrase "animal spirits," which is basically an emotional narrative that's believed by millions of people. These spirits range from a lack of confidence in leadership to a mass exodus from markets out of fear of losing money. In the view of economists like Shiller, this kind of emotional intelligence is often based on irrational fears. We get scared, so we start running in one direction or another and start doing ignorant things (e.g., the smartest investors are *buying* in down markets to get bargain prices, not selling).

When it comes to the job market, though, developing emotional intelligence is essential for survival. You can't stay anchored to the status quo or that you provide an irreplaceable service. We need to keep an open mind, even when it comes to negative outcomes.

HOW PEOPLE REALLY CREATE

Since "AI will be a far more formidable competitor than any human," Hess opines, what do we need to do to compete in the "frantic race to stay relevant"?[94] As I've detailed earlier, a focus on the higher-order skills that fuse the Quad I attributes into a creative whole is a basic premise. You can't be open to a new role in the workplace unless you have an open, creative mindset. But there's more to it than just thinking differently.

A lodestone of creativity is *emotional engagement.* Why do something you don't care a fig about? I know, hundreds of millions slave away at jobs that are mind-numbing. That's been the case since the dawn of the machine age and the punishing curse of the industrial revolutions. Yet suppose you somewhat like your job or are just staying with a gig you don't like to keep the health insurance or other benefits. Should you quit to do something you love? Even as we face massive unemployment, why is part of the advice matrix "follow your bliss"? Well, honestly, for some, it's a really bad idea, especially if you're hoping to hold onto a job doing something that's going to be replaced by a robot. Yet part of building emotional intelligence is navigating the space between what we *want* to do and what we *need* to do. We need to go beyond our skill set to find something purposeful that will give us a reason to go to work—and try something new. That's hard to do.

Surely, in becoming a Quad I, you need emotional drive in addition to the ability to improvise, innovate, and employ critical thinking. Here again, though, Hess sees a fly in the ointment:

> The challenge for many of us is that we do not excel at those skills because of our natural cognitive and emotional proclivities: We are confirmation-seeking thinkers and ego-affirmation-seeking defensive reasoners. We will need to overcome those proclivities in order to take our thinking, listening, relating, and collaborating skills to a much higher level.[95]

What kind of "collaborating skills" is Hess referring to? The ability to integrate our utmost creative skills with the analytic/big-data processing power of AI. And here's where we invite our humanity inside of this crowded room. We'll not only need to be better listeners with our coworkers and students, we'll need to be attentive listeners to what *data* is and isn't telling us. Instead of constantly seeking approval for our work, we need to be able to accept failure and go back to the drawing board. Every time we take this humble route, our brains are automatically rerouting neuronal circuits: we're learning most from falling on our faces. That means parking our egos *outside* of our workplaces and our own little bubbles.

I'll leave this chapter with a story about my father. As I began this book, he descended into dementia. He was a retired schoolteacher, band director, and musician. When he started to crash his car and do odd things, I got angry at him for all sorts of reasons. But he couldn't help what he was doing since his mind was fracturing. It wasn't until I realized that *I* needed to dock my ego that I could begin to provide the services he needed. I was massively humbled and became both parent and caregiver. My role changed from son to guardian and advocate. It was painful but necessary. Hundreds of millions will go through this experience—*and* joblessness— but learning isn't achievable until you let humility be your teacher. When the narrative changes, you need to see things in a new light. That's creativity in the most pragmatic lens.

FINAL NOTES

For many, the narrative on automation varies widely, depending on who's telling the story. The exploration of the human psyche is part of this story. How do we think? How important are emotions? What will AI truly take over and where will it come up short? Predictions on what will happen when are doomed to be unreliable, so you need to take a meta-view: some skills will be highly automated, while others requiring Quad I traits may not be.

We need to keep an open mind on our jobs and skills. It's essential to have emotional intelligence. It's detrimental to be anchored to one narrative about our industries and professions. In the next chapter, I'll explore how we can combine human with machine skills to create a synergistic work environment.

EIGHT

The New Integration: How Humans Will Interface with Robots

Every company that is technology-driven from Amazon to Tesla Motors is embracing the robot age in every aspect of their operations. But there will be opportunities where humans will play a unique role in mega-automation—they will work in a cooperative role. This chapter explores that brave new world of a *New Integration*.

I'm back at the University of Chicago again, only speaking myself on a panel sponsored by the college's Graham School, where I've taught a few classes. The topic at hand is the importance of the humanities in business. I'm joined by Christian Madsbjerg, a global consultant and author of *Sense-making: The Power of the Humanities in the Age of the Algorithm*, who is delivering the keynote. The moderator is Prof. Mark Miller, an English professor at the university. Other panelists include Don Phillips, a managing director at Morningstar, the financial information company; David Kalt, an entrepreneur and founder of Reverb.com, the online musical instrument marketplace; and Jan Perrino, the founder of Perrino Associates and former McDonald's executive.

Even in the automation age, the liberal arts will help us understand and help us thrive working alongside smart machines. Liberal arts and the humanities in particular aid us in understanding narrative. From Homer to machine learning, we need some perspective to see where we've been—and where we are going. We're entering a *New Integration*, one that merges culture, history, and the humanities into our tech-centered reality.

Madsbjerg is one of those multidisciplinary thinkers whose interests span the globe. He stresses the importance of "culturally intersubjective thinking." In order words, how can we make sense of the world without using culture as a context? Technology is one of many tools, but it doesn't give us comprehensive answers. It can't "explain" hip-hop, social media, or memes. While it can track narratives and mountains of data, it can't give us that broader perspective that infuses observations and analysis with meaning. Curiosity and employing a broad base of knowledge found in the liberal arts help us construct meaning out of our experience.

"And while a liberal arts degree isn't required for this type of ability," Madsbjerg observes, "it happens that most people who can think in this manner do have one. In America today," he notes, "we're stripping away context and not putting it back together, and I think there's a great need in corporations to have people who know how to do this. When it happens, it is intensely successful."[96]

While technical skills will help us work with machines, they are not the Rosetta stone for giving us context in our jobs. Coding will open up some doors, but the skill alone isn't enough. Kalt, who has more than 50 computer engineers working for him, discovered that those with purely technical backgrounds didn't necessarily make the most insightful employees.

"Having hired hundreds of software developers over my career," Kalt said, "I have found that the best software engineers, the best leaders, the most creative types are *all liberal arts educated*." He added that his chief operating officer at Reverb, who manages 50 engineers, earned a degree in philosophy from the University of Chicago.[97]

Even when it comes to numbers and financial information, coding and technical knowledge isn't enough. Don Phillips was one of the first employees of Morningstar, a global financial information company that does everything from manage money to rating mutual funds. He's truly a pioneer, working as one of the first employees of Joe Mansueto, the founder, who launched the company in his Chicago apartment. Don is a liberal arts kind of guy who earned his master's degree in English literature from the University of Chicago. Since I've known Joe and Don, from the inception of Morningstar three decades ago, I can say they are broad thinkers with diverse interests. You can spark a conversation with Don about *Moby Dick* and in the same breath discuss some of the best mutual fund managers in the world. He's focused on narrative, but he's not *all* about numbers or analysis, which is the bedrock of financial analysis. He can tell you a story about anything—and he's a good writer. Narrative skills tell the tale behind numbers, and they are derived from the liberal arts. The emotional intelligence behind a saga is something that can be nurtured over a lifetime.

"They're skills that shine over a long period of time," Phillips said. "The concepts behind finance aren't too difficult. We can teach the math, but we can't teach you empathy and writing skills."[98]

The New Integration will involve an array of skills. It may be that knowing poetry or line drawing will be just as valuable as knowing predictive analytics. Having studied Plato and Aristotle may be just as powerful as understanding cybersecurity. Yet it's even more important to know how all of these knowledge skill sets *synergize* that will make a profound difference in the automated workplace. It's not like sampling a buffet and filling yourself up. You need to know how an entire meal is cooked—the history of the cuisine, the ingredients, the seasoning, etc.—before you can put the feast on the table. That translates into understanding major components of human behavior and intellect.

WHAT HUMAN TRAITS ARE NEEDED IN THE NEW INTEGRATION?

Right off the bat, it will help tremendously if you have a little coding and some machine knowledge under your belt. Then you'll need to employ your imagination to solve problems. Creativity isn't a solitary intellectual tool—it's a whole interactive toolbox that is fueled by other ideas.

Andrew McAfee and Erik Brynjolfsson, two MIT scientists, are on the leading edge of the New Integration. Coauthors of *Machine Platform Crowd* and *The Second Machine Age*, their writing has sparked widespread rethinking of the changes occurring as the workplace scales up to automate. Although they have given multiple warnings on what massive automation means to a largely unprepared populace, they are also optimistic:

There's never a better time to be a person with the skill, talent or luck to produce a good that can be delivered via the global digital infrastructure. . . . One of the things our economy needs most are people who specialize in inventing these new jobs. This task requires designing and implementing new combinations of technologies, human skills and other resources and assets to solve problems and the needs of potential customers. Machines are not very good at this sort of large-scale creativity and planning, but humans are.[99]

Human skills matter, yet they are like multilayered ingredients in our feast of knowledge. Yeast isn't just a powder that makes dough rise. It's a colony of microorganisms that produce carbon dioxide and other by-products. Salt isn't just a seasoning; it's sodium chloride, something we need for metabolism. Similarly, there are several brain elements that make creativity rise.

Martin Seligman, in his groundbreaking book *Homo Prospectus*, looks deep inside the human psyche to examine the essential building blocks for a Quad I in the New Integration.[100] Central to Seligman's research is the concept of *prospection*, which is "imagination about possible futures."[101] Without imagination, or the ability to see other realities, creativity is stuck at the starting gate. Creativity builds on drawings, dreams, and fantasies, yet can be fueled by originality as well. See any Hollywood blockbuster. None of the effects or monsters are real. But they come alive on screen thanks to a combination of imagination and tremendous computing power and animation. Here are some key parts of that process, according to Seligman:

Imagination. What makes us human allow us to create "mental imagery of things that may or may not exist; counterfactual conjecture; alternative pasts; daydreaming; fantasizing; pretending; mental stimulation of other minds; mental rehearsal and aspects of night dreaming."[102] In short, you need to be able to harness your preteen mind and take on some of the skills of a novelist or sci-fi writer. Machines don't create alternate realities out of whole cloth.

Fluid Reasoning. This is the brain tool that allows you to deal with things as they happen. Suppose some driver turns into your lane without looking or your child has a fever or your roof develops a leak? We're able to respond because we combine insight, experience, and the ability to improvise. You're able to react to a situation and the environment in real time.[103]

Crystallized Intelligence. This is a store of knowledge that accumulates over time.[104] It's a tool to deal with people and situations based on experience. It's the police officer responding to a domestic disturbance call, a professional athlete dealing with injuries, and Pablo Casals playing the cello in his ninth decade. It's wisdom and the ability to access and apply knowledge.

Short-/Long-Term Memory. These are experiences that we store every day and over the years. Some of us are better with short-term skills, other on long-term. My father had better access to his childhood memories while not remembering where he lived or the names of his children. Computers, of course, are exceptionally good at the memory business, but they may not be able to relate it to a task at hand.

Visual/Auditory Processing. Yes, machines can do facial and pattern recognition, although they may not know what they are looking at; appearances such as expressions can be deceptive. While computers may be able to recognize Bach, Beethoven, Nirvana, and Kanye West, they may have no idea what they are listening to or what the music means. Like general memory, of course, these abilities slow and decline with age, which is an opportunity in the New Integration. We can use machines to see, perceive, and think better.

Quantitative Knowledge. This is where machines clearly have the upper hand. Millions can do math in their head, although not as fast as computers. It's important to know what coding means and what it can— and can't—do. The digital age is swimming in programs and formulae. It's up to us to make ethical and socially responsible decisions with the data and its various forms of manipulation.

Emotional Intelligence. As noted earlier, this is the ability to incorporate our feelings into our worldview. Can we separate the two like Mr. Spock, the timeless half-Vulcan, half-human character? Not easily, although emotions can power the passion behind creativity, invention, and innovation. You may have seen people suffer and die from cancer or heart disease, so you're compelled to work on a cure.

Unstructured Cognition. I know this sounds wonky, but this is the catch-all for letting your mind wander or just goofing around. It's the pickup basketball game or doodling, a visit to a museum or trail walk. Or, as Seligman observes, the "ability to generate original ideas, as well as actual creative achievement, is associated with diffuse, unfocused attention to the external environment."[105] Yes, daydreaming and fantasies are healthy. Sure, machines can do random patterns, yet can they have bizarre dreams that result in movies like *Blade Runner*, based on the Philip K. Dick story "Do Androids Dream of Electric Sheep?"

Intuition and Slower Thinking. In the athletic world, think sprinters and long-distance runners. The fast processes, called "System 1" functions, react quickly: think a lion coming at you. The "System 2" functions require analysis and executive function.[106] We're weighing facts on a jury before rendering a verdict. The quick part of our brain is more closely linked to emotion and survival, while the slower engine is much more reasoning. Computers can do both fairly quickly without the emotional connection.

As you can see, we're pretty complex thinking machines. We need to react to our environment, our emotions, what we know, and what we create in our minds. All of these traits make us whole human beings.

AUTOMATION SNAPSHOT: ROBOT FARMWORKERS

Can a robot pick a ripe raspberry or strawberry without bruising it? For thousands of years, humans have been cultivating the land. Some of it has just been unrelenting, hard labor involving thousands of farmhands. Then along came reapers, tractors, hydraulics, and diesel engines. Now the percentage of Americans who work on farms is minuscule.

Yet it still takes thousands of workers to pick certain kinds of crops. Massive combine harvesters can handle grains such as wheat and corn, even when piloted by robots using GPS systems. The smaller the fruit or vegetable, though, the more you need the human touch, although that will change. As the pool of migrant laborers shrinks, it is driving increased automation.

A consortium called Harv, representing large growers and local farmers, is pooling cash and resources to automate harvesting particularly for smaller fruits and vegetables.[107] It has a tall hurdle: humans can pick about 80 percent of crops without damaging produce. Machines need to be able to do delicate work, which involves mechanical finders that are gentle and probing. That takes a surprising amount of processing power and mechanical articulation.

In the case of agriculture, the push to automate is driven by economic trends. There are fewer workers who are earning more money. And industry is always on the route to increase productivity. As machines drop in price, they begin to compete favorably with human labor. After all, machines don't need to be paid overtime, yet will still need maintenance and supervision. "Automation is the long-term solution, given the reluctance of domestic workers to do these jobs," Tim Richards, the Morrison chair of agribusiness at Arizona State University, told *The Washington Post*.[108]

HOW WILL THE LIBERAL ARTS HELP US INTERFACE WITH MACHINES?

The intrusion of machines into labor is going to require a new mindset. You'll not only need technical knowledge, but the openness to embrace new ways of thinking. That's not easy for most people to do, especially as they cling to their biases and worldview. That's where the liberal arts can open doors.

Leonardo, for example, not only saw himself as an artist, he was an anatomist, designer, and engineer. He was working on solutions to move water and make better weapons. Michelangelo was not only a painter and sculptor, he was an architect whose designs were incorporated into St. Peter's Basilica in Rome. Even modern-day designers such as Frank Lloyd Wright and Frank Gehry infuse art into architecture. Wright's trip to Japan and Germany profoundly influenced his aesthetic and "prairie style."

What are the liberal arts, and why are they important? They are built on the foundation of *openness to experience*. "Individuals who are open to new experiences are more likely to make connections among seemingly unrelated pieces of information, as well as see new patterns," notes Seligman.[109]

The definition of liberal arts goes back to the fourteenth century and was the foundation of academic learning. Derived from the Latin *liber*, meaning "free or unrestricted," it was then (and now) a novel form of learning where you would explore new ideas in science, philosophy, the humanities, and mathematics.[110] The core of liberal arts was what the Greeks and romans called the *trivium*, which was grammar, rhetoric, and logic (basically reading, writing, and philosophy). Over the years, this core curriculum expanded to the *quadrivium*, which added arithmetic, geometry, music, and astronomy.[111] Of course, when the scientific revolution emerged in the sixteenth and seventeenth centuries, the liberal arts umbrella widened even more to include biology, chemistry, physics, and a multitude of spin-off science and technical realms such as electromagnetism. evolution, genetics, and thousands of subspecialties.

What makes the liberal arts unique is that while you're building on past knowledge, you're guided by philosophy and often allowed to break the rules and come up with new ones. You're asking questions, not just learning an old set of rules. Contrast that with strictly professional regimens such as business, engineering, and law where often the rules of a profession may be sacrosanct. Liberal artists are more in the business of seeing the world in a newfangled way. They are trying to make *sense* of the world in their own fashion. There is no program that allows them to experience what Aristotle called *phronesis*, an "artful synthesis of both knowledge and experience," Madsbjerg observes.[112] This is the cornerstone of what I referred to earlier as synergistic creativity.

Culture and meaning, what Madsbjerg calls "thick data," occupy center stage in a world in which human experience is more important than an obsession with technology. Creativity and "bottom up" inductive reasoning may help us even more. We need to *interpret* rather than blindly accept the changes around us. We question instead of passively consume. We challenge what we hear, see, smell, and taste. We're employing critical thinking. He calls this process "sensemaking," or using the liberal arts to understand what's happening. He observes:

> Today's world feels overwhelmingly complex because we are obsessed with organizing it as an assembly of facts. Big data makes us feel as though we can and should know everything there is to know on earth. But this is a fool's quest, and it leaves everyone feeling depleted and lost. . . . The tools of navigation have always been available to us. But we must take responsibility for interpreting them.[113]

Novel experiences can be motivating. Suppose you like opera or David Bowie, hip-hop, contemporary art, or free jazz. That excites circuits in your brain. You're motivated to explore. If you have grit—or the stick-with-it-ness to follow something through—you'll discover something new. That why language, art, the sciences, literature, and cross-disciplinary knowledge are the bedrock of innovation in the New Integration. Finding a way to work with machines may be informed by reading *Frankenstein* or *Faust*. Or a basic knowledge of Egyptology or the history of Luddites in the early Industrial Revolution. There is no pat formula for how all of this fits together.

Even better is combining the talents and experiences of working in groups. Harriet Zuckerman found that "two thirds of the nearly 300 Nobel Prize laureates named between 1901 and 1972 received the prize for work done collaboratively."[114]

HOW WE WILL BE SMARTER THAN AI

If digital systems and AI will be able to do hundreds of millions of jobs efficiently and won't demand paid vacation or any time off, where does that leave us? How can we think about a world in which machines can *outthink* us on nearly everything?

There's a philosophical maxim called Polanyi's paradox, named after the philosopher Karl Polanyi. Simply put, it calls into question the prospect of automating something *that we don't fully understand.* We're not quite sure how we can define "being human." There's still a lot of work that needs to be done on how the brain works, when life begins, and how the environment interacts with our bodies. While we can create digital and even quantum models of neural networks, it's still nowhere close to the real thing. Human understanding is still this strange mix of culture, experience, family, and emotion. How do you program that?

As T. L. Andrews writes, "we cannot program what we don't understand."[115] Activities like painting a picture, dancing, or writing a persuasive essay—and deciphering their meaning—may be beyond the reach of digital comprehension. It's really tough to come up with an algorithm that interprets or even understands Stravinsky's *Firebird* or Alan Moore's graphic novels. Andrews notes that understanding complex human activities is relative:

> True, there is evidence that machine learning capable of "understanding" such tasks tacitly might eliminate this hurdle, but for the time being, professions that require flexibility and creativity are quite resistant to obsolescence. In the short term, the main effect of automation will not necessarily be eliminating jobs, but redefining them.[116]

Andrews's suggestion on how we redefine jobs? A "strategic investment in education," which I'll examine more in the next chapter.

In order to succeed in the automation age, we'll need a deep sense of the importance of liberal education. And that doesn't mean that everyone should have a liberal arts degree. In the New Integration, that means using the humanities to understand and adapt to our data-centric environment.

At the expense of sounding extreme, it will be an epic battle to keep up with the rapid quantum leaps of AI. Governments like China are devoting tens of billions of dollars to dominating AI, fueling "the next great technology race of our generation," says John Allen, president of the Brookings Institution, a national think tank.[117] Allen proposes a "U.S. national education strategy" that would ask the following questions:[118]

1. **What Will Be the Implications for How We Educate, Train, and Develop Teachers?** A discussion on the impact of AI on education will point dramatically to those who facilitate the process in our schools. The very term "teacher" may be insufficient to adequately capture the role of this key individual in the educational experience. Ultimately, the critical question will be "are the teachers of today ready to develop the leaders we will need tomorrow?" A difficult question, to be sure, and the answer today is no.

2. **What Will an AI-based Classroom Look Like?** *With AI, every aspect of the traditional learning environment is up for reimagining.* Will the classroom continue to be a physical space? Or will it be a virtual "space" using networked augmented or virtual reality technologies? The answer is yes to both, and the student in tomorrow's AI-based educational experience will be exposed to an immersive, digital education heretofore unimaginable.

3. **What Will This Kind of System of Education Do to Reduce Inequalities in Our Society?** Local governments, schools, and especially the private sector will need to routinely intersect to create synergy and symbiosis to enhance our educational processes. Through the AI-powered digital space, "opportunity for all" may become a reality for those who previously had little means of achieving their own piece of the American Dream.

Note that Allen is *not* calling for banning computers or digital learning from classrooms. He's *not* saying that book or experiential learning is obsolete. He's calling for us to reenvision education itself because "we are not training our young leaders with the tools required to be successful in the digital age, and that has deeply troubling implications for the future of American society."[119]

Of course, overhauling our education isn't possible until we understand and chart out the possibilities of the New Integration. It asks us to shelve the idea that AI will totally eliminate the need for human intelligence, labor, and emotion. While the "Robot Apocalypse" or "singularity" (machine intelligence surpassing human smarts) is still possible, there are no limits to our education—and we must transcend them.

FINAL NOTES

We need to embrace a wide variety of experiences and learning to survive and prosper in the age of automation. That means accepting the foundational guidance of the liberal arts, particularly the humanities.

What does this mean in practical terms? We still need to tinker around, daydream, and fantasize. We need to invent our own narratives and interpretations of the world. While big data and AI are certainly powerful tools, we need to step away from them to ask our own questions. It won't hurt to look deep into culture and history for the answers.

Most of all, we need to use the tools that have already been given us: fluid and crystallized reasoning, the ability to think fast and slow. The quick responses of our minds won't beat those of a digital intellect, but our slow thinking and synergistic creativity can combine emotional intelligence with a deep sense of humanity. We will all need a philosophy of ourselves, technology, and the things that concern us. Education is the key.

The New Integration combines so many things in human knowledge, it's a real hodge-podge. It's fun and imagination. It's life-giving and challenging. Yet there's another level to it—knowing what we *need* to know (education)—that's a crucial step in the age of automation. That's what I'll be exploring in the next chapter.

NINE

Bot Busters: What to Do to Prepare for the New Convergence

This chapter presents a summary of what we need to know about the future of work. How can everyone best prepare for it? What kinds of education will be best?

The Fox Lake Park District hall is full of environmentalists, activists, retirees, local officials and those just interested in a discussion on climate change. Leading the meeting is Rep. Brad Schneider, my congressman and friend, joined by Mayor Donny Schmit, mayor of Fox Lake, and several representatives of village government and nonprofit groups. It's a chilly February day as we watch snowmobiles skitter across the frozen expanse of Fox Lake, one of several lakes in Northwestern Lake County (Illinois) that's part of an interconnected chain of glacially created and river-fed lakes. Climate change couldn't be a more important topic here as epic floods ravaged and destroyed homes in 2017. Here, surrounded by water nearly everywhere you go, any change in water levels threatens home, recreation, and clean water supplies.

"The 2017 floods caused some $1.8 billion in damage," Mayor Schmit notes, "most of that outside the floodplains. Our infrastructure today isn't able to handle the storms of today and tomorrow."

As I write this, the United States—and most industrialized countries for that matter—is far behind the curve in addressing global warming. Greenhouse gases are pouring into our atmosphere at a rate sufficient to produce 5.6 billion tons of carbon dioxide by 2050.[120] In real terms, those heat-increasing emissions are enough to make storms more violent, flooding more prevalent, wildfires/droughts more devastating, climate out-migration more pronounced, and to create a public health crisis so catastrophic that it will become a new pandemic of sorts.

In the automation age, global mega-issues such as climate change will elude the best AI programs. It will be nearly impossible to automate solutions to the causes and effects of rising global temperatures, which scientists almost universally concede are triggered by human-driven burning of fossil fuels.

There are myriad approaches to solving this existential crisis, which is already making some places uninhabitable due to excessive heat and rising sea levels. And it goes beyond science. It's observable fact that even as countries fumble to enact uniform climate change policies, glaciers are melting, low-lying coastal areas are being inundated by seawater, and catastrophic storms and wildfires are consuming entire towns.[121] Even inland storms that flooded my hometown in 2017 are beyond what anyone could anticipate. The present, aging infrastructure is not able to handle extreme weather. This is not a machine problem, yet it begs for a big-data, big-policy application and lots of Quad I types who have a broad range of experience and education to tackle these complex problems. It calls for *convergent* thinkers who look at systems and systems of systems.

In Fox Lake, for example, water flows from the Fox River from Wisconsin into the chain of lakes in Illinois. That brings millions of cubic yards of silt and agricultural pollution, which eventually fouls the water flowing across the Wisconsin border, then feeds into the Mississippi River, finally pouring into the Gulf of Mexico. Examining the local water issues really means understanding the impact of a watershed that stretches nearly 2,000 miles. You need to understand how the system works. It's complex.

Not all systems can be fully understood by science, engineering, and math, though. Policy makers, political leaders, academics, ethicists, the clergy, historians, and philosophers need to get on board in a *New Convergence.*

WHAT IS THE NEW CONVERGENCE?

As noted in the previous chapter, we're going to need to fire up our liberal arts and humanities thinking and combine it with technical and scientific knowledge. We need data and analysis, but we also need narrative and sound policies. We're facing some mammoth problems that require interdisciplinary thinkers. The New Convergence gets them in the same room in an intellectual scrum. And those huddling in this new intellectual mashup need to employ synergistic creativity.

The common thread in the New Convergence is that it puts many diverse ideas on the table. It gets away from algorithms and can get messy. Imagine a religious scholar arguing with a data scientist. Or a climate change expert plumbing the knowledge of a geologist or philosopher. There is no one worldview anymore. It's a polyglot of ideas that's mixed together. According to the National Science Foundation, this convergence is the following:[122]

- Convergence research is a means of solving vexing research problems, in particular, complex problems focusing on societal needs.

- It entails integrating knowledge, methods, and expertise from different disciplines and forming novel frameworks to catalyze scientific discovery and innovation.

- Convergence research is related to other forms of research that span disciplines—*transdisciplinarity, interdisciplinarity, and multidisciplinarity*. It is the closest to transdisciplinary research that was historically viewed as the pinnacle of evolutionary integration across disciplines.

- It's *research driven by a specific and compelling problem.* Convergence research is generally inspired by the need to address a specific challenge or opportunity, whether it arises from deep scientific questions or pressing societal needs.

- *Deep integration across disciplines.* As experts from different disciplines pursue common research challenges, their knowledge, theories, methods, data, research communities, and languages become increasingly intermingled or integrated. New frameworks, paradigms, or even disciplines can form sustained interactions across multiple communities.

- From its inception, the convergence paradigm intentionally brings together intellectually diverse researchers to *develop effective ways of communicating across disciplines by adopting common frameworks and a new scientific language,* which may, in turn, help solve the problem that engendered the collaboration, developing novel ways of framing research questions, and opening new research vistas.

Translated from sciencespeak, convergence is about diversity of thought and education. Can a biologist talk with a policy maker? They normally don't, but should. Should an AI scientist talk with an oceanologist? Absolutely. Where *deep integration* comes in is a need for specialists to learn and absorb new disciplines. Data analysts might delve into anthropology, for example.

WHAT DOES NEW CONVERGENCE EDUCATION LOOK LIKE?

Having laid out the argument for convergent problem solving, how do we educate people to start thinking this way? What will you need to know in the New Convergence? As I write this, there are only a handful of educators in the world who understand what's happening. They are adapting their classrooms and curricula. It's happening very slowly. Higher education has been stuck in an ossified way for hundreds of years. Although you might learn many things—some of them useful—in elementary school and college, once you get into a degree program, you are forced into one discipline. It's even more regimented in graduate and professional programs.

Conventional education is often based on how well you regurgitate facts on a standardized test. It's not centered on *how* you learn or flexible modes of problem solving. And it's not about convergent thinking. Think silos and tunnel vision. It's the wrong kind of education to make people competitive in the automation age.

Cathy Davidson, an education innovator and author of *The New Education*,[123] is not afraid to launch a withering critique of modern education, which is rooted more in industrial factory thinking than convergent realities. She's found that the mainstream educational system evolved from 1895 to 1925, then, for the most part, stopped evolving.[124] It morphed from universal education during an era of agrarian progress to training people for the industrial age. That paradigm, of course, is outmoded in the digital or "gig" economy, where careers and industries are unstable and likely to be drastically downsized by AI and automation. Information is readily available and manipulated online; you can even get degrees and nearly any course on the Internet. Knowledge of all stripes is widely dispersed through search engines and public databases of academic papers. So why, in this global information age, are educators still insisting that students memorize facts and take multiple-choice tests?

> Students need a new way of integrating knowledge, through reflection on why and what they are learning. They don't need more "teaching to the test." They need to be offered challenges that promote their

success after graduation, when all educational testing has stopped. This is an engaged form of student-centered pedagogy known as "active learning." Students are encouraged to create new knowledge from the information around them and use it to make a public, professional or experiential contribution that has impact beyond the classroom.[125]

Davidson's "active learning" means engaging directly with the world instead of being immersed in textbooks and advanced placement courses and tests. She also favors ending grading and exchanging it with experiential learning, interactivity with teachers and other students, and an emphasis on writing and communicating. Instead of students being passive consumers of facts and equations, they'd be explorers, *discovering* what they don't know.

Yet education culture is granitelike. Most parents and teachers don't realize the extent to which they are still pushing rocks uphill. "What do you plan to major in?" is one of the most common questions asked of 18-year-olds, but it's patently unfair. The better question should be "what do you want to learn?" or "what problems do you want to tackle?" Here are some other key ways of retooling education with critical questions. I would ask educators to pose these questions (for exercises on reeducating yourself, see the appendix):

1) What do you want to fix in the world?

2) Where would you go to learn something bold and innovative?

3) What do you really need to know to understand a complex problem?

4) What's outside of your comfort zone that you want to confront?

5) Where would you find purpose and meaning in learning something new?

Like any New Convergence approach, the best place to start is through philosophy, that is, asking questions such as the ones I've just listed and coming up with a theory of what you want your work life to look like.

PROBLEM SOLVING AND DESIGN LEARNING: ATTRIBUTES FOR NEW LEARNERS

Aging populations, infrastructure repairs, and climate change—among dozens of other global problems—demand a new kind of education. Simply focusing on what's always been taught in the liberal arts will not be

AUTOMATION SNAPSHOT: ZORA THE CAREGIVING ROBOT

We all love good—and bad—robot stories. Ever since Hollywood latched onto this theme, it's been the source of endless movie plots. I don't know if such a survey exists, but I'd wager there are more nasty automatons than friendly ones in cinema.

Let's go with the amiable robot for now. Can they truly be companions or help us when we're most vulnerable? In France, researchers are experimenting with "Zora," a tiny robot with two arms and legs who offers companionship to people who have dementia and need 24-hour care.[126] These patients in a long-term care facility, with limited cognitive abilities, are also in need of someone to visit them. While Zora isn't a substitute for a caregiver or relative, the robot will play games and lead exercises. Like Tesla's robot boat, Zora is controlled remotely, usually by a nurse with a laptop.

Zora is treated like a doll of sorts, with residents cradling the robot and cooing and kissing it. It's almost like the robot is a child in need of attention. Although the robot's functions are extremely limited—it can't dispense medication, change diapers, or prevent patients from falling—it's one step in a growing trend to supplement care for the very old.

As industrialized countries get progressively older, there will likely be a shortage of health-care workers to serve this population. To date, Zora Bots, the Belgium-based manufacturer of robots, has sold more than 1,000 of the robots to long-term care facilities around the world. Other manufacturers such as Sony are following suit.[127] According to a report in *The New York Times*:

> In nearly every country, the population of older adults is rising. The number of people over 60 will more than double to 2.1 billion by 2050, according to the United Nations. The figures point to an emerging gap. There simply won't be enough people for the required health care jobs. Proponents argue new technology must be created to help fill the void.[128]

Aging populations present a double-edged social dilemma. While there will be a pressing need for more hands-on human and social services workers, will there be enough people in these professions to fill the need? Will automation step up to fill the gap? The answer probably lies in a hybrid approach, with humans working alongside robots as partners to solve everyday problems.

enough. A New Convergence education will demand flexibility, emotional maturity, and the ability to pivot to a changing society and workforce. Problem solving is placed higher on the educational tier than rote learning. Think less about tests (if you have to think about them at all) and focus on building something new within a group.

To gain a New Convergence education, explore what's coming out of Stanford's *Social Innovation Review*, which is attempting to "reboot" the

American high school. If conventional education isn't suitable for the information age, some changes are due in classrooms around the world. Based on the premise that American high schools are based on a model dating back to 1893, Silicon Valley pioneers are overhauling grades nine through 12 for today's demands to produce Quad I's.

Patrick Cook-Deegan, a lecturer at Stanford, and Bob Lenz, executive director of the Buck Institute for Education, have been working thoughtfully to modernize the American high school based on neuroscience and "purpose learning." They surmise that 65 percent of jobs today's students will have don't exist yet, which is derived from a U.S. Dept. of Education study.[129] That means that whatever high schools are offering now isn't adequate to prepare students for an evolving labor market.

Yet adolescent brains—and those of most adults for that matter—aren't prepared for this reality. They are unfocused on the future, beleaguered by endless testing, and unsuited to "know what they want to do." What's a better fit for the teenage mind? Design thinking, which emerged from Stanford as a core principle in Silicon Valley inventiveness.

With design thinking, what you need to create isn't in some textbook and is unlikely to be found in an advanced college placement course. It's only through brainstorming, creating, and building that young minds find a path to the future. Of course, being Silicon Valley-based, Cook-Deegan and Lenz put a premium on engineering, which combines math, science, and applications to come up with solutions. Another linchpin of rebooting schools is finding *purpose*. Millions of students are sitting in classrooms learning the same material everyone else is, but why are they doing it? That's a question conventional education is loath to answer. Purpose provides some direction, which is what the researchers hope to instill in young minds in their "Project Wayfinders."

> "Purpose is a stable and generalized intention to accomplish something that is at the same time meaningful to the self and consequential for the world beyond the self," notes Prof. William Damon, a professor of education at Stanford.[130]

What makes for a better learning environment is a concentration on mindsets, skills, and emotional habits that build confidence. Here's a shortlist of those attributes from the Stanford group:

- **Mindsets.** The best learning environment promotes growth, creative confidence, sense of purpose, and embracing failure. In other words, students will need a tougher skin to know that they can take risks, fall on their face, and learn from their experience. What anchors their identity as learners is a "self-defined sense of purpose." What do they want to learn? What do they hope to accomplish?

- **Integrative Skills.** They should be able to visually communicate, employ design thinking, manage their time, be leaders, and exercise self-control and discipline. For many, this simply means the ability to work alone and with others and accomplish many tasks. Part of success is not only productive collaboration, it's the ability to finish a project and show and tell others what you did (remember "show and tell" from grade school?).

- **Good Habits.** They should be able to meet and talk with mentors, meditate/reflect, write in a journal, read news articles, exercise, and do "active shaping" to improve learning conditions. This is an overall life balancing. It's not enough to study, design, and learn. You need to exercise your mind and body in other ways and find some sense of inner peace. It's important to feel gratitude for your work and feel good about yourself.

- **Good Traits.** This is where behavior comes in. Part of what shapes successful learners is their sense of self and regard for others. It helps to be compassionate, a good listener, energetic, motivated, positive, hardworking, and worldly. All told, they should be able to work in a team and make the kinds of contributions that will move a project forward.[131]

What do these ideal New Convergence students have in common? They engage social intelligence to a higher degree. Unlike Tesla, Edison, or Darwin slaving alone with their work in a single room or lab, they are immersed in a group experience. They have to build things by complementing their skills and personalities with those of others. They should also have a credo. This is a like a set of religious tenets; it's something you need to believe in order to move forward. Here are 10 attributes that Cook-Deegan and Lenz say are vitally important:

1) Boldly Experimental. You are action oriented and have a willingness to fail.

2) Deeply Grateful. You have a humble appreciation for people and the world around you.

3) Instinctively Purposeful. You chart your own pathway with a self-defined vision.

4) Intuitively Collaborative. You are a relationship builder who constantly seeks guidance and support from diverse perspectives.

5) Keenly Self-Aware. You know what nourishes and sustains you.

6) Fiercely Determined. You persevere and keep on track despite many obstacles.

7) Globally Minded. You are invested in your community, nature and the world around you.

8) Fluidly Adaptive. You can find multiple ways to the same objective.

9) Insatiably Inquisitive. You think independently and are driven to pursue knowledge and the truth.

10) Integrity. You stand firmly rooted in your values and will courageously act on them.

If you're hoping to find your way in the automation age, these 10 attributes are key strategies in a workable game plan. Although all computer programs have specific rules, this rubric gives you some flexibility. Knowledge is always a good thing to acquire, but you'll always need to add those philosophical elements to the mix. You'll need a set of values and the gumption to act upon them. Thinking globally and acting locally still makes sense. Having a moral and intellectual compass will keep you on course.

THE NEXT ESSENTIAL STEPS IN A NEW CONVERGENCE EDUCATION

I don't want to suggest that our society is completely unprepared on the education front for the New Convergence. Over the past 20 years, some schools have adopted the Project Lead the Way program, which combines design, coding, and preengineering skills. The program's Activity, Project, and Problem-Based (APB) Approach "centers on hands-on, real-world activities, projects, and problems that help students understand how the knowledge and skills they develop in the classroom may be applied in everyday life. The APB approach scaffolds student learning through structured activities and projects that empower students to become independent in the classroom and help them build skill sets to apply to an open-ended design problem."[132]

I've had a chance to see Project Lead the Way in action in my daughter's high school. In the first phase of the program, students are asked to build simple things like wooden swords. Then, as they use computer-aided design tools, they can build more complex objects—in teams. By the end of the program, educators hope that graduates will aspire to continue their education in college engineering, computer, and design programs.

Basic design and coding courses are based on the idea of *complexification*. You learn by starting out simple, then proceed to increasingly more layers of complexity. Beau Lotto, the author of *Deviate: The Science of Seeing Differently*, writes that the process of complexification is part of the ecology of innovation: "Start simple (few dimensions), add complexity (more dimensions) and then refine (last dimensions) through trial and error . . . and repeat."[133] This is how most of Silicon Valley operates. Keep at the problem until you find a solution. That's the learning method found in programs like Project Lead the Way and in most research and development centers across the globe.

Where do you go for a well-rounded New Convergence education? If your high school is fortunate enough to offer Project Lead the Way or similar design-based courses, that's a start. Community colleges, as I noted earlier, will offer more vocationally based programs that range from preengineering to specific skills like robotics integration and digital manufacturing.

A third option is to find an *employer* who will train you, which is becoming increasingly prevalent as the new workforce is demanding diverse skill sets that are not taught in schools. Whatever path you take, don't believe that one, narrow degree or specialty will provide you enough of a foundation. Although those with a college degree will likely make more money than those without one, it's no guarantee.

"More students enroll in college, but the share of 25-year-olds with a bachelor's degree stands barely above the 1975 level," observes Oren Cass, a senior fellow at the Manhattan Institute.[134] The reality is that college has become too expensive for many middle-class families, and college completion rate takes five or six years for those who are unprepared. As result, students have racked up more than $1.6 trillion in college debt.[135]

Is the educational system coming up short because students are not testing well enough or getting top grades? Are they failing to achieve basic goals? This has been a common criticism of education in the industrial age. Students just can't make the grade for any number of reasons. They include too many video games, not enough reading, not enough social interaction, and poor math skills. While many of those shortcomings may have something to do with students being unprepared for college, they are bromides that don't reveal the flaws in a test-based educational system. And I'm hardly being scientific in these observations. The reasons for underperformance are complex and can fill many volumes. Academic success, though, is not always an indicator of vocational achievement.

Adam Grant, an organizational psychologist at the University of Pennsylvania's Wharton School, has found that "academic excellence is *not* a strong predictor of career excellence . . . grades rarely assess qualities like creativity, leadership, teamwork skills, cr social, emotional and political intelligence."[136]

This is good news for "B" and "C" students. It's often not *what* you know, but how you acquire knowledge that counts. Those who are taking a dozen advanced-placement college courses in high school may not be any better prepared than those who don't take them. That's because what you need to know about making things, solving problems, and working with people isn't generally taught in schools. You have to get down into the trenches to figure these things out. It would be ideal if these skill sets were in textbooks. Yet much of what you need to know is experiential and not learned from a PowerPoint or book.

One concluding thought for the New Convergence: you need to get dirty out there in the real world. Yes, get stuck in the mud. Climb your way out of a hole. Fly a plane when all the red lights are on. Fail and move on. That also means stepping away from conventional education and work. Get away from the computer and social media. Put your smartphone in a drawer for a day. Don't watch cable TV and don't work on another project on your home computer for a while. Meditate. Mingle. Play with Legos or a board game. Take a stroll outside. Forget about education and your career.

"One of the worst things you can do for your innovative capacity," advises Michael Platt, a neuroscience professor at the University of Pennsylvania, "is to sit at a computer punching numbers into an Excel spreadsheet, or writing Goleman emails. . . . So stepping away from your computer and getting up and walking around—taking breaks is really important for stimulating innovative thinking."[137]

The New Convergence is going to be a renaissance for those who are dabblers, explorers, tinkerers, inventors, and garage experimenters. They are taking journeys into the unknown. Sometimes they break things and put them back together. Other times they are just driven by what they don't know and point their handmade telescopes to find new comets. They are willing to take on big ideas like climate change mitigation or small ones like making a better hand tool. They don't quit and they manage to find a way to work with others. They are not invested in finding the perfect solution or getting the best grade. The experiment is their life, and they are willing to fail to find what they need. Maybe they will pick up a new language or build a musical instrument. No matter what they do, they have some inner direction. The journey is everything, and they don't get stuck in ruts. They are discoverers. Acquisition and application of knowledge is more highly prized than achievement and acquisition of wealth. Are you a new convergent thinker?

FINAL NOTES

The New Convergence is going to be painful for those who aren't prepared or for those who ignore its emerging realities. The evolving workforce will not only demand that we work alongside robots and various artificially intelligent tools, we'll need to have the personal flexibility to adapt to new roles. You will need to have a moral compass with values that include curiosity and compassion. You will also need to be able to work in groups and understand how to design something.

What's important in the New Convergence is a presence of mind and a willingness to fail. You've long forgotten about the tests you took and the grades you got. What did you learn from the projects you took on? What did others bring to the table? How did you add to your skill set? What did you acquire that made your stronger and more adaptive?

In the next chapter, I'll show how all of these skills add up to a whole person who is able to adapt and transform themselves to prosper in the age of automation. It's a joyous journey.

TEN

The Joyous Journey: How to Prosper in the Automation Age

You'll need to follow a knowledge- and experienced-based path to
have a productive journey. This is a summary and road map of what
you'll need to know and do.

I am in a gorgeous conference room in a corporate headquarters. I can't
exactly tell you where I am because I'm little more than a fly on the wall.
I'm not really supposed to be writing about what I'm about to hear. I'm part
of the proceedings. It's a secure location and there are no journalists in the
room, nor would they be necessarily be invited. (I'm a journalist by trade,
but I'm not in the room covering the event).

Floor-to-ceiling windows beckon to the forest setting outside of the green
(environmentally engineered) building, which has an airy atrium with a coffee shop, trees, and a fountain. If I was still immersed in corporate life—
or starting a career—this might be a sublime place to work. People don't
appear to be drones here and casually sit down in comfortable nooks with
their computers to work. It seems on the serene side. There's even an
employee store as you walk into the main entrance (that isn't even marked
with a single sign), selling some of the company's most popular products.
It's more of a cavernous cathedral of commerce than an industrial hive.

An executive in the company, a woman charged with recruiting, is giving us a pitch on their ideal employees. The $10 billion-plus company is
engaged in e-commerce and selling millions of products, so they need
people who are not only educated but can pivot to do new things for jobs

that may not exist now. They have more than 300 openings to fill, yet are struggling to find the right kind of employees. I ask her some questions on the kind of background and personality types she's seeking.

"They should be intellectually curious and nimble," she replies. "They should be cross-functional and be able to do data analytics and have a well-rounded business acumen."

I then translate her corporate speak into words that make sense to me. She's sounding like a lot of corporate recruiters these days, using the same jargon. Basically, her ideal employee should be data-centric— analyzing numbers for meaningful trends—but be able to see business solutions from a number of perspectives. That's the flexibility factor I've been expounding in previous chapters on becoming a Quad I. While she may be looking for someone with a business, accounting, economic, or technical background or degree, she's open to liberal arts majors. Now we're talking.

"They should also have an entrepreneurial spirit," the executive continues, "and be comfortable with change as part of solutions. They don't have to stay in their lane nor always stay with the same team. They should have a diverse talent and be the best version of themselves."

If you've ever been to a business motivational talk or read any self-help book, this language is loaded with clichés, of course. Sure, we *all* want to be our best selves! What is this executive really saying? She wants employees willing to take a journey and develop their minds, but they will need the kind of attitude that will allow them to adapt. For me, to hear this from a recruiter from a big, sophisticated company selling millions of products was an affirmation. Yet how does one adapt? Start the journey with some baby steps, but be principled in your approach.

ACCEPTING THE FACTS ABOUT AUTOMATION: WHAT WE'VE LEARNED

You wouldn't start a trip without having an itinerary, travel guide, or online maps, would you? The same logic applies to charting a course in the increasingly automated labor market. Just as you wouldn't assume that jobs that have existed for centuries will still be around, you also shouldn't assume that what you know now will be enough to prepare you for this journey.

Here's a summary of what I've discovered and how you can use it in your work road map:

Millions of Jobs Will Disappear. They won't go all at once, but they will slowly evaporate—like water from the ocean. Some, in manufacturing, are long gone, while others will succumb to the slow drop of AI. Here are some scenarios from earlier chapters:

- Researchers' estimates on the scale of threatened jobs over the next decade or two range from 9 percent to 47 percent of the current workforce.

- The jobs that are threatened by automation are highly concentrated among lower-paid, lower-skilled, and less-educated workers.

- The activities most susceptible to automation are physical ones in highly structured and predictable environments, as well as data collection and processing, according to a McKinsey study. In the United States, these activities make up 51 percent of activities in the economy, accounting for almost $2.7 trillion in wages. They are most prevalent in manufacturing, accommodation and food service, and retail trade.

- It's not just low-skill, low-wage work that could be automated; middle-skill and high-paying, high-skill occupations, too, have a degree of automation potential.

- The Oxford University model in the introduction predicts that most workers in transportation and logistics occupations, together with the bulk of office and administrative support workers, and labor in production occupations, are at risk.

Innovation Will Drive Automation. From ancient times to modern industrial society, machines have been invented to reduce the need for human labor. The growth of mega industries has driven the economic imperative to make more things with fewer hands. This trend will accelerate as AI is integrated into nearly everything companies do. That means low-skilled jobs are most vulnerable. There will be more automated cashiers in retail settings and self-driving vehicles. Even easy "gig" economy jobs are likely to be automated.

Logistics operations like warehousing and transportation will also see high degrees of automation as robots take over human jobs. Notes technology writer David Pogue, whom I cited earlier: "Robots are definitely going to take over millions of our jobs. About 5 million retail jobs, 3 million truck driving jobs and 500,000 taxi and ride-sharing jobs could, in time, take their place alongside the millions of factory jobs that robots have already displaced."[138]

Anything Repetitive and Formulaic Will Be Automated. This broad category includes anything from back office clerical work in insurance, legal, or other administrative functions to certain forms of journalism such as earnings reports. This includes any task from filling out forms to company earnings reports. If it can be replicated a million times—and it's just a matter of inserting data—machines will be able to do it. That means anyone writing basic reports that don't require extensive analysis will be replaced by machine learning. Even legal forms handled by lawyers and paralegals are being automated. Machines are even "robo-signing" credit documents. Although formulaic repetition is something done best by algorithms, the tasks that don't need much human intervention are the most vulnerable to be automated.

Middle Managers, Professionals and Financial Service Workers Are Vulnerable, Too. Even if you're *not* doing simple, repetitive tasks, computer programs can read X-rays and MRIs, trade stocks, and assemble investment portfolios. How many jobs are imperiled by the growing ability of machines to sort through ever-complex reams of data? It's hard to say, but this is a frontier that is being breached as back offices and middle management are being automated.

Machines Will Be Able to Do More, So You Do Less. The ongoing evolution of automation technologies will enable machines to "see," "hear," and analyze images as well as data. These new machine skills already include facial recognition and biometric data such as retinal scanning for security purposes. Robots will be able to know where they are going, so they can better navigate factory and warehouse floors. Tools such as predictive analytics and neural nets are allowing computers to forecast and think like analysts. They will eventually be able to do coding and make decisions based on crunching big data. Again, this imperils data-centric jobs from insurance claims adjusters to clerical workers of all stripes. If there's any situation in which data can be stored, analyzed, and processed more efficiently by machines, that doesn't bode well for job security.

Integrated Innovation Is a Bright Spot. Any job that demands merging new ideas, critical thinking, invention, and improvisation is unlikely to be automated. This new role for human workers entails working with and alongside machines, letting them handle the data-centric tasks while people ponder the big picture and make decisions. Creativity is driving this new kind of worker, who will need a broad skill set to prosper.

Becoming a Quad I Is Essential. The four pillars of prospering in the automation are **innovation, integration, insight, and improvisation.** These are the parts of a whole person who needs to be able to think on the fly, look deep into a problem, and work with machines to come up with something new. I know this is a tall order, but millions are already doing these things, although they may not know it. Artists and performers do this all the time. Anyone who has ever worked on a project that's empowered to come up with a new product or novel way of doing things is also in this realm. They are all creative, yet they are using their human skills to innovate.

You Can Acquire and Develop Quad I Skills through Social Labor Ecosystems. It's rare that anyone is born a Quad I. The good news is all of these skills can be learned and nurtured. Most metropolitan areas have social ecosystems that are called business accelerators or incubators. There's plenty of help to get you started in a business or social venture. Most community colleges will assist entrepreneurs and solo businesses. Through collaboration with experienced professionals and businesspeople, you can develop your Quad I skills.

Synergistic Creativity Is the Core of the Quad I. While a skill set is certainly important, what's the fuel behind your engine of growth? It's the ability to work with others, to make and break things, and to fail. This is how we learn. You'll also need to develop higher-order abilities to tinker, troubleshoot, and problem solve. Synergistic creativity, in short, is melding hands-on knowledge with a path toward a solution, big or small. It's taking thousands of pieces of data or physical parts and assembling something in the real world, whether it's a 3D printed chess piece or an artificial limb. It's working with machines to make something better. Whether you pick up some new skills learning coding online or venture into a maker space or fab lab, synergistic creativity is a productive mix of assembly, math, programming, visualizing, and just having fun creating something for the first time.

Essential Mind Skills Will Aid You Greatly. Yes, prospering in the automation age is all in your head, but don't forget your emotions as well. You'll need emotional intelligence to cope with the coming changes. You'll not only need a narrative—*where do you want to go, what do you want to learn*—you'll need the social intelligence to reach outside yourself. Then you'll need relational reasoning to judge where you've been and where you need to go. Sometimes the story we tell ourselves dominates our life and worldview. Do you want to prosper? Change your narrative.

Embrace the New Integration. Even if you've gone deep into coding or other technical skills, you'll need a broader background that has nothing to do with the technical world. The New Integration has a warm place for the humanities. Literature, art, music, and the social sciences can still inform us about our place in the automated world. Sure, machines will juggle and analyze trillions of data points, but what does it all mean? That leaves plenty of room for personal/social philosophy and ethics. What questions should we be asking? What precedents have been set in history? What does art tell us about our humanity? The New Integration can show us where we've been and cast some light on where we're going. We'll also need to look deep inside ourselves and how our brains work and reimagine education along the lines of how we learn over time.

The Bot Busters Are Within You: Enter the New Convergence. It's not easy to change or to accept that you need to know more than you know now. Yet I'm convinced that the New Convergence will allow us to be more human and let machines do most of the tedious work that doesn't fully engage us. How do we get where we need to be? Knowing and engaging in design thinking is a start. This involves working on projects with a diverse group of people, accepting failure and shortcomings, and having the ability to see things in a different way. That means experimenting, being grateful, and being relentlessly curious. It also involves a high degree of humility. No one expects you to be a pioneer in every venture you undertake; you need to give yourself permission to try something and move on. The key to this kind of education is to change your way of thinking. Knowledge and book learning aren't enough. It's a journey with a lot of side trips.

10 ROUTES TO PROSPERITY IN THE AUTOMATION AGE: EMOTIONS MATTER

The road ahead is going to be challenging and full of potholes. You'll need to demand more of yourself and be able to integrate with others. Assuming that you don't have a self-driving car to our destination, winning the robotic workplace involves a set of self-improvement exercises, affirmations, and new skills. You'll need to be passionate about change; here are 10 ways to make that journey go smoother:

1) **Be Humble.** There isn't a better way to start out. Even if you think you have the perfect road map, the ideal degree, or a whole toolbox of synergistic creativity, you'll still need to apply yourself. You probably won't have a "one and done" degree or career. I'm not sure that they exist anymore in the smart machine age (SMA). As Edward Hess and Katherine Ludwig, professors at the University of Virginia, note in their book *Humility Is the New Smart*, you'll need to admit that you'll have to *work* at critical and innovative thinking, emotional and social intelligence, and being creative. "We'll have to change the behaviors that inhibit our abilities to excel at SMA skills. . . . For most of us, these behaviors require that we radically change how we negotiate the world."[13] The researchers have distilled these essential behaviors to four traits: *quieting ego, managing self, reflective listening,* and *otherness.* Assume you know nothing about a subject, place, or person. What's the best approach to gain knowledge? Listen and learn. Shelve your ego. Ask questions. Reflect on the answers. Know that others aren't where you're at. Empathize. Put yourself in their shoes. These four skills don't come easily for most people. And just admitting that you need to be quiet and listen carefully is a profound first step. When I first starting caregiving for my father, who fell into progressively deeper stages of dementia over the past few years, my ego got in the way. I took his mental incapacity personally, and it made me angry. Once I put my ego in a box, I was able to care for him and provide him what he needed. What I gained in knowledge—and I hope compassion—prepared me for my journey ahead.

2) **Try to Make Sense of Your World.** Yeah, right. With big data, climate change, automation angst, global political turmoil, and information coming at us 24/7, how likely is it that *anything* makes sense anymore? Yet what makes us human is that we operate on narratives. Is it that automation will make us slaves to robots or free us for the things that engage our souls? What opens the door to a new story? Being open to ideas, as I illuminated in the opening section of this chapter, can welcome new insights, the core of being a Quad I. "Whether it is the experience of running, the ritual of putting pen to paper or the tortured exercise of imagining knives, creative thinkers

all develop techniques to keep themselves open to ideas," advises Christian Madsbjerg in "Sensemaking."[140] Not surprisingly, that's what writing and art attempts to do. Vincent Van Gogh saw the night sky a whole lot differently than Rubens. James Joyce saw his journey radically differently than his contemporaries Hemingway and Fitzgerald, although all were directly involved in reinventing themselves and literature around the same time. Every poet, painter, sculptor, or designer wants to do something new. To get in the zone of synergistic creativity, sometimes you need to have a new pair of intellectual glasses. Even if your lens makes for fuzzy vision, it helps to be open to new experience.

3) **Collaborate.** Although the history books are chock-full of lone geniuses like Leonardo and Tesla, it takes more than a village to foster new ideas and products. Steve Jobs had the immensely talented team at Apple to realize the iPhone, iPad, and other revolutionary devices. It takes a large team to design a new robot, building, or city, for that matter. And all of those architects, engineers, designers, and policy makers need to work together. Think of the complexity involved in just building a skyscraper. A structural engineer needs to figure out stress loads and ensure that it will withstand high winds. Hordes of other team players have to design everything from elevator shafts to toilets. They all need to talk to each other. I suppose that robot designers are programming certain social skills into machines, but will automatons ever have an innate desire to work with other robots or loath certain workers? "We humans want to work together and help each other out and we can and should be encouraged to do so," note Andrew McAfee and Erik Brynjolfsson in *Machine Platform Crowd*.[141] Even if you think you're the most introverted person in the world, join a team. That will give you some perspective on your strengths and weaknesses and how you can contribute. Teams will be ever more powerful in the future as we tackle some of the most difficult problems facing us.

4) **Reimagine Your Own Education.** Is there such a thing as a perfect education? Well, if you see it as a moving river, no. It's a fluid experience, coursing its way to the oceans. You will need a novel kind of training where computers handle most of the heavy lifting of objects and data. Just having a little coding under your belt is a good beginning, but you need to go beyond that. It would help to understand what

AI and machine learning are all about. Know their strengths and weaknesses. They are evolving technologies, so that requires constant reading to keep up with the latest and greatest software and hardware. It would be useful to peruse *Wired* (magazine or online) or MIT's *Technology Review.* Keep up with what's coming out of Stanford on design thinking. Did you know you could build your own curriculum? You could save a lot of money by taking online courses (thousands are available), picking up a class at a community college, or signing up for certificate programs through trade associations. "It is vital that we re-imagine our educational institutions for a world where AI will be ubiquitous and students need a different kind of training than they currently receive," write Darrell West and John Allen of the Brookings Institution.[142] How can you possibly keep up with the latest trends in technology and science? Focus on what's important to you. What do you want to know? What do you *need* to know? Think lifelong learning. Your education doesn't stop with a diploma.

5) **Be an Entrepreneur.** I know not everyone feels comfortable with starting their own business. You are chief cook and bottle washer doing your own books, making a product, offering a service, and doing marketing. But you can think like an entrepreneur and start out small. A side pursuit like selling handicrafts or writing apps might get your feet wet. To take your enterprise to the next level, you'll need to build your knowledge, experience, and skills. There are thousands of online courses you can take and millions of instructional videos. In that sense, we're in the golden age of self-instruction and so many are teaching online that you don't need to spend six figures on a college degree to pick up incremental knowledge. "Entrepreneurship will gain importance in the age of AI," add Anastassia Lauterbach and Andrea Bonime-Blanc in *The Artificial Intelligence Imperative.* They conclude that the "fusion of technology and human-centric sciences will enable the development of new industries and educational fields."[143] Do you think even the smartest machine can venture out into the world and see a niche that needs to be filled with a human service or new app? *Entrepreneurial thinking is all about seeing a problem and trying to solve it.* Of all the traits in the New Convergence, this may be one of the most solid cornerstones.

6) **Think about Big Problems.** This is where our species needs the most help. How do you supply freshwater to places where it's scarce? How

can you cure cancer without debilitating the patient? How do you provide clean sources of energy? How do you keep rising sea levels from inundating coastal cities? All great ideas start with seemingly mammoth problems. Everything from windmills to gigantic dams came from identifying needs for large numbers of people. It helps to be guided by history. Until the Industrial Revolution, the bulk of humanity was involved in hunting/gathering and agriculture. It took a lot of time, labor, and persistence just to survive. People didn't live very long, and life was really tough. Now with modern medicine, our greatest challenge may be the best application of our energy and labor. If machines are going to do most of the grunt work and data crunching, that leaves the age-old problems of curing seemingly uncurable diseases, clean energy and water, preventing war and securing the peace, and economic opportunity and equality for billions of people. Of course, we'll have to work together in new ways to tackle these issues. To make this journey successful, an unprecedented cultural and political shift is in order. As Jeremy Rifkin posits in his *Third Industrial Revolution*, the new world order will move billions of people toward a shared prosperity—in theory. "We will need to be prepared by reading the human race to shift out of an industrial existence and into a collaborative future just as our great-grandparents made the shift from an agricultural and rural existence to an industrial and urban way of life."[144]

7) **Values Matter.** Maybe the job that will be least prone to be automated is that of ethicist. These are the folks who, based on grounding in philosophy, religion, logic, culture, and science, tell us whether we're on moral high ground—or not. Should we be tinkering with genomes to make the perfect child or sterilizing mosquitoes? When should we edit genes to eliminate or add a trait like blue eyes or red hair? Should we ever give robots the authority to engage in warfare without our supervision? I could list a hundred questions for which we don't have good answers, yet they need to be asked and discussed. What's important to you? You'll need to look deep inside and examine your passions. If you want to tackle regulating AI or tackling climate change or online privacy, those are certainly good subjects in which to invest your passion, time, and intellect. What about gene-editing and "designer" babies? To what degree should we be messing with nature and evolution? What's the downside? Keep in mind that even the most

mundane areas such as policy making are loaded with opportunities. The tougher the subject, the more your human skills will be needed. And you'll need to be optimistic about engaging in these incredibly difficult realms of society and technology. "We need to think much more deeply about what it is we really want and what we value," conclude MIT professors Brynjolfsson and McAfee in their book *Second Machine Age*, which examines work and prosperity in a time of rapid automation. "Our generation has inherited more opportunities to transform the world than any other. That's a cause for optimism, but only if we're mindful of our choices. Technology is not destiny. We shape our destiny."[145]

8) **Sharpen Your Critical Thinking.** Sure, it's easy to love the latest AI gadget that will let us hurl voice commands at a smart speaker and obtain everything from our favorite pop songs to ordering merchandise. But what information are these machines gathering on what we want and what we buy? Are they listening *all the time* to our conversations with loved ones? How are they monetizing what they hear? How do we protect our privacy? Most technology is value neutral: AI interfaces are gathering and analyzing information. They are not making judgments, but we should. You'll need to have a keen sense of what doesn't seem right, then create an argument around it. This is a higher-order skill honed in debate clubs and modern politics on every level. The Hewlett Foundation, which created a Deeper Learning Network, notes that critical thinking and problem solving should be a prime skill for everyone, particularly students. "They should know how to find, evaluate and synthesize information to construct arguments. They can design their own solutions to complex problems."[146]

9) **Communicate.** You could be the most astute, brilliant person when it comes to technology or intellectual skills, yet if you can't tell anybody about yourself or ideas, you might as well be living in a cave. Communication is not just about writing, speaking and visual presentations: It's also about reaching others on an emotional level as well. I can't tell you how many PowerPoint slides I've seen where after the first five minutes I just wanted to leave. The presenter didn't communicate anything to me and often panicked if they had technical issues. They couldn't just tell me what that really wanted to say; they were simply reading some gibberish off a slide. That's not communication.

As I explained in my chapter on narratives, we have to be able to tell stories and connect with our audience. What do we want to convey? Why are our ideas important and different? Why do we matter? Speaking clearly and briefly is more effective than presenting 100 slides. You've lost people after the first five slides anyway. Tell a story. Tell *your* story and how you came to your subject. They don't want more statistics. They want more *you*. Writing is also critical in sharing your knowledge and ideas. Concise, jargon-free prose always makes a difference. Don't be afraid to be funny, silly, or ironic. We love goofy twists in plot lines. Imagine you're explaining something to your grandmother—in your own words. By the way, the best essays are truly personal ones that tell people who you are in your own voice. Machines may pick up how to write in your *personal tone*, but they won't know your narrative. You should own that. More on this subject in the appendix that follows!

10) **Lifelong Learning Rocks.** No matter what age you're at—or *think* you're at—when you stop learning, the machines will catch up to you and whatever you were doing. I know that sounds paranoid. There's a simple explanation: your knowledge is like the foundation of a great building. It's in the process of building that you learn, not in assembling the materials. You can be self-directed or obtain many degrees. Whatever way you do it, keep in mind the components of becoming a Quad I. You will always need to improvise and integrate while gaining insights into what you're doing. There's a lot of information sitting out there on servers. Until you learn what something means to *you*, it's meaningless. The best thing about lifelong learning is that it has no limits and can be completely customized to your personality and passions. Be curious. Be bold. Find out what it means to be human. It can be filled with pain, sorrow, and failed expectations. Yet in every case—every single moment—you will have the unique opportunity to learn something new. It will sustain and enrich you. Don't be afraid to think and learn big. "Thinking big is a way of life," remark Tony Wagner and Ted Dintersmith in *Most Likely to Succeed*, a seminal book on reinventing education. "Failure is embraced and resilience is rewarded. Out-of-the-box approaches are admired, not marked down."[147] Yes, despite what you've heard, failure is a good thing. It's really how we learn—if we choose to engage in insights that build us up.

GAINING A BETTER UNDERSTANDING OF PROSPERITY

How does one prosper when machines can think and eliminate our jobs? Most of society is tragically unprepared for a workforce that's highly automated. That's a question that policy makers, ethicists, economists, and thinkers across the world are grappling with as they envision the future of mass unemployment.

One idea that's gained favor in recent years is guaranteed or universal basic income (UBI). The main assumptions behind this universal payment to everyone is that there will be millions who will be unable to cope or pay for basic living expenses. Not everyone can be trained or reeducated to survive in a world in which AI will eliminate tens of millions of jobs. Not all of us will be able to embody my Quad I traits. That means rampant economic inequality will force millions to the margins. You can't be prosperous if you can't pay the bills or have a disposable income.

Economist Thomas Piketty, along with hundreds of other thinkers across the world, sees universal basic income as a safety net in the automation age. The concept addresses the question "what about the people who can't or *won't* be retrained to do higher-order skills?" What are they supposed to do if they can't find work? Ideally, UBI ensures that they won't starve and won't be able to make ends meets in the gig economy.

"For all those without jobs, or who only have a very part-time job," writes Piketty, "or indeed whose job is divided between multiple small employers or contractors, then there is no other solution than to pay the universal income in the form of an allocation managed by public agencies."[148]

While paying everyone a basic income sounds like the simplest solution to a complex problem, it may not address the reasons we work in the first place: *labor often gives us purpose and meaning.* Sure, you can argue that history is littered with repetitive and meaningless jobs where people worked in dark, dangerous factories or toiled endlessly in fields. Automation has clearly vanquished most of those tasks and will continue to do so. What about the *need* to work, to engage your body, mind, and soul in something purposeful? Will a basic income give them an incentive to find something rewarding?

Max Tegmark, an MIT professor who has examined the role of humans in the context of the advances of AI, digs into the idea of humanity needing work to maintain well-being:

Jobs can provide people with more than just money. Voltaire wrote in 1759 that "work keeps at bay three great evils: boredom, vice and need." Conversely, providing people with income isn't enough to guarantee their well-being. . . . So precisely what valuable things do jobs contribute beyond money, and in what alternative ways can a jobless society provide them?[149]

The answer to Tegmark's question is a journey of the soul, best navigated by your mind and heart. Take the first step and keep on going.

FINAL NOTES: EMBRACING MINDFUL OPTIMISM

If you want to prosper in the robotic workplace, you need one more mindset that machines will never have: mindful optimism. This attitude puts you in a place to see the future *you want* while having the flexibility to transact positive change.

As Tegmark suggests in *Life 3.0*, being a mindful optimist "is the expectation that good things will happen if you plan carefully and work hard for them."[150] Although I'm not sure how you can plan for changes in the workplace that haven't happened yet, you can use most of this book to become the kind of Quad I person who will have the tools to pivot and do new things. Tegmark elaborates:

> To be a successful mindful optimist, it's crucial to develop positive visions for the future. When MIT students come to my office for advice, I usually start by asking them where they see themselves in a decade. If a student replies "Perhaps I'll be in a cancer ward or in a cemetery after getting hit by a bus," I'd give her a hard time. Envisioning only negative futures is a terrible approach to career planning! [151]

How do you develop a positive vision that's a fulcrum for change? Tap your passions in a way that you can collaborate and communicate to others what you want to do to make the world better. Embrace what you don't know. Don't be afraid to start a new venture if you can't see what you want in today's workplace. Keep on learning. Make a friend of failure. Think big, but be humble. Engage others in your dream. Think of how many others can celebrate your vision. You're not alone, so make it a party.

Afterword

I am asking a question of Aaron Elster, who lived through the Holocaust hiding in an attic in rural Poland. Although all but one sister perished, he survived when a Polish couple hid his sister and himself in their country home.

It's not the least bit unsettling that Aaron answers my question about why he's talking about his experiences even though he's not in the room with me. I am querying an artificially intelligent (natural language) interface linked to a holographic image of Aaron, who died several months earlier. His programmed response is that we need to be "upstanders" to resist intolerance, persecutions, and future genocides. It's his enduring mission and that of the Illinois Holocaust Museum, the first institution to employ this kind of technology.

Aaron is the future in a peculiar and important way that merges automation with intelligence, history, culture, and often current events. His image and thousands of his responses will be there for the present and future generations. We should never forget the murder of 6 million Jews, in addition to millions of gypsies, disabled persons, and dissidents because the technology will be present to tell us his—and many other horror stories—that far too many choose to ignore.

The awkward collision between technology, work, and memory is going to be rough. No one will be untouched. As the AI exhibit in the Holocaust Museum demonstrates, technology can be a powerful force in helping us to remember. Yet we must keep in mind that we need a solid, nuanced, and complete cultural perspective when we use technology to illuminate our past, present, and future.

Let me be clear: in no way am I comparing the automation age to the Holocaust. I'm only saying that everyone's life will be profoundly impacted in this hyperlinked industrial moment. We will need to ask some essential questions about work and humanity to avoid the horrors of the past. In the intersection between now and the future, we will need to be present to realize our full humanity, which is a continuing saga. When we lose sight or awareness of our collective soul, horrible things can happen.

What do history and our experience and that of our family mean to us? It's hard to march forward if you don't know who you are. You can access billions of images and words on social media and online sources, but it won't give you a sense of where you can be in the world. In that sense, technology may provide more noise than meaning (see the following appendix for comprehensive exercises that will help you avoid inner and outer noise).

There's so much noise out there it would be an understatement to call it cacophony. Everything from beauty videos to hate speech: so much so that when some of it gains currency, it can make someone a multimillionaire— or murderer. The power of this ubiquitous technology is that its power is unfettered. Although social media companies have made feeble attempts to police it, how do you keep an eye on the most virulent and violent actors when billions are using the medium 24/7? These companies even refuse to call themselves "media" companies, which strikes me as a dodging of their responsibility to curb the worst of the worst postings.

Of course, in an amoral tech world with few or no rules, anything can happen. A terrorist mass murderer can post a video of his killing and hateful manifesto for all to see, which is what happened in a massacre of 50 people at prayer in New Zealand. Other hate crimes were perpetuated. Then we get stuck in this tired debate of whether we're chilling free speech if we start to regulate images of murder and racial violence. Where does it stop? And what will happen when AI can furiously replicate and even create its own propaganda? And what about all of the false narratives being generated every moment of the day online? Who's doing the critical thinking to police or fact-check these lies? There will never be enough watchdogs to go around, and government can only do so much.

All of this noise can be harmful to our minds and souls. We clearly need some ethical boundaries, but don't hold your breath waiting for Silicon Valley to be its own policing agency. When your paycheck depends on promoting technology and gathering data for advertising, such a function will either be given insincere lip service or not happen in a meaningful way.

There is some hope that tech giants are being somewhat reflective. As I was finishing this book, Stanford University announced the formation of an Institute for Human-Centered Artificial Intelligence.[152] Organized to "inculcate in that next generation a more worldly and humane set of values than those that have characterized it so far—and guide politicians to make more sophisticated decisions about the challenging social questions wrought by technology"—the institute will be playing catch-up. The Pandora's box was opened a long time ago.

Yet the onslaught of AI, social media, and multiple modes of communication creates a panoply of opportunities. We will need enlightened ethicists and government officials to make policy for this data- and image-driven craziness. They will have to know communications, history, law, philosophy, technology, and be open to many possibilities (sounds like a Quad I to me). And they will have to work with others to achieve some reasonable goals on regulation that will protect our treasured free speech principles and public safety. I know that's an incredibly tall order, but no one government agency has tackled these issues. There's no protection of privacy in the U.S. Constitution. Nothing (at this writing) precludes a company from using our personal data to enrich themselves or a global corporation. While social media may be "free" to consumers, what is the cost to society? We all pay when information is abused or leads to mass murder. We will clearly need a new set of laws and regulations to protect us and prevent abuses.

Technology alone isn't a solution to any of this. It's an amoral set of tools. It can facilitate our distractions and save labor, but it won't erase history or the darkness of the soul. We need to remember that. Like anything born of a factory or science, the evolving thinking machine age needs to be supervised and policed. We can't forget where we came from, which is never easily discovered in a search engine or AI interface. We have to know who we are and where we are going. Until then, we will be lost in a perilous digital jungle of our own making.

Appendix: Exercises for the Automation Age

How do you become a Quad I and prosper in the age of automation? You'll need to practice at what you need to become. Take it a step at a time. But don't be discouraged. I'm offering 10 ways and specific paths to acquire the skills you need. Do them a bit at a time. I wouldn't even look at the entire list in one sitting

Don't do a linear read: scan through the list and pick out something you'd like to learn or accomplish. This is a smorgasbord, not a one-course meal. My suggestion is you start with some fundamental things you need to work on: You need to communicate better? Start in that section and work through the questions. Be honest with yourself and don't be afraid to mess up. Take your time. Here are some basic exercises. Enjoy!

1. **Find Out Where the Job Growth Is and Get the Training You Need.**
   This is the most basic exercise and the simplest one to do. My best source is the U.S. Bureau of Labor Statistics, which tracks the labor market in great detail. Since you already know from previous chapters which jobs are likely to be automated, head in another direction. Generally, the more a job pays, the more training and academic background it requires, particularly in the technical and scientific fields. That may mean computer or basic science degrees coupled with courses in math, analysis, and statistics. Health science professions—at least the highest-paying ones—are no less rigorous. And those with advanced professional degrees tend to command the highest wages. The backgrounder section (below) will give you a sampling of where the job market is going, although there are no long-term guarantees.

Questions to Ask:

A. What industries will be hiring the most in the future?
B. What long-term trends will be driving the hiring?
C. What skills and training will I need to qualify for the best jobs?
D. Which jobs are likely to pay a living wage?
E. Where can you get the training or degrees you need?
F. How can you best utilize your knowledge and talents?

Table 3   Backgrounder: Top 10 Fastest Growing Occupations

Job	Growth Rate	Median Pay
Solar panel installer	105%	$40,000
Wind turbine service tech	96%	$54,000
Home health aides	47%	$23,000
Personal care aides	29%	$23,000
Physician assistants	37%	$105,000
Nurse practitioners	36%	$104,000
Statisticians	34%	$84,000
Physical therapist assistant	31%	$57,000
Software developer/apps	31%	$101,000
Mathematicians	31%	$103,000

Source: U.S. Bureau of Labor Statistics Occupational Outlook Handbook.

All annual medians are based on surveys through 2017, but are projecting growth through 2026. While these occupations are showing robust growth in the short term, a number of factors could influence their standing on this list, so it pays to keep in mind longer-term trends.[153] In most cases, unless you already have the needed background, you may need to get more education.

"Education . . . is both the greatest weapon we have against the Robocalypse and the best tool with which we can equip our population to be productive and engaged members of society," writes Jason Schenker, author of *Jobs for Robots, Between the Robocalypse and Robotopia.*"[154]

2. **How to Focus on "Soft" Jobs.** Not every job that will endure will require an extensive tool kit of technical, scientific, or math skills. Some

jobs will exist because they require "soft" skills of directly engaging with other people. Some of these jobs are predicated on your personality, but not entirely. Patience is important in the soft skills. Some of the toughest jobs require the ability to step back from one's self, evaluate the situation, and take a deep breath. Or they may require the kind of focus on mind and body that's intense and sustaining. Since AI doesn't involve being directly in the physical world—remember this is virtual intelligence based on code—it can't really "be in the room with someone." Sure, maybe a device can learn how to listen to someone or even gauge the severity of their pain or injury, but it will be awfully hard for it to read between the lines to tell what's really going on. That's higher-order thinking.

Questions to Ask:

A. What "soft skills" do you have in dealing with people?

B. Can you do "active listening," where you're able to listen and analyze without making judgments?

C. Are you able to convey knowledge in an accessible way, that is, can you teach what you know?

D. Do you have some extraordinary physical skills, for example, strength, agility, endurance? Are you a competitive athlete?

E. Are you able to "work a room" to meet, greet, and engage with a variety of people?

F. Do you have enough patience to deal with children or adolescents or special-needs students?

G. Can you deal effectively with people with severe physical. emotional, social, or mental issues?

H. What can you offer (among all of the above traits) that will enable you to do specialized work?

BACKGROUNDER: FIVE SOFT SKILL JOBS THAT ARE UNLIKELY TO BE AUTOMATED

Please note: none of these jobs are "soft" or easy. When I refer to soft skills, I mean that these professions are mostly nontechnical, although all of them involve some degree of data analysis and general computer skills. They won't be going away and will be more important than ever.

Teaching. Having taught as an adjunct lecturer in various colleges, I know how hard this work can be. I have enormous admiration for preschool, elementary, special education, and high school teachers. You need to be patient and understanding while working within a set of rules. I know there's a lot of software engineers who think this can be automated or replaced with online learning—some of it will be—but a great teacher changes lives. It's still a noble, though difficult, profession with lots of teachers retiring.

Professional Athlete. It's extremely difficult to get paid to run, jump, shoot a basket, puck, or kick a ball. Millions try, but they will never be the caliber of a LeBron James or Tom Brady. Only a tiny percentage will ever receive a college athletic scholarship and need to be a professional prospect to get a full ride. Humans really need to play and watch sports. Maybe it's a healthy metaphor for waging war, but it engages us on so many levels it's not going away. There is no online or video game equivalent to watching a real hockey, football, baseball, or soccer game. So we will need extraordinary athletes who not only entertain us, they inspire us to aspire for more.

Politician. I know a lot of you will instantly grimace at this, but politicians actually serve a useful purpose. Since I am one (I'm a county commissioner as I write this), I'm engaged in creating and gaining acceptance for new policies on the environment, taxes, and governance. In a democracy, we're empowered to work with all kinds of people to find solutions. We're trying to do problem solving on issues like global warming, fixing roads, and paying for these social goods in a responsible and equitable way. Sure, there are a lot of dark forces in this business, a subject that can and will occupy several volumes. But the bottom line is that this is one of the purest human service professions that we know. Figuring out people and what they truly need—and helping them—is hard and challenging work. It can also be rewarding. Enlightened people can write good policies. Better politicians need to be well educated and attuned to a diverse array of experiences.

Judges and Juries. Justice is another one of those human endeavors that engage nearly every part of our humanity. Most of us are not able to peer into people's minds and souls, so when they do something wrong, we need to make judgments based on a set of laws. Those rules, established over centuries, are constantly changing. And no one civilization ever gets it right. Being able to apply these rules and mete out punishment is something that's essential in an equitable society. There is no one formula that works every time, and we often get it wrong. Yet in the end, the most imperfect human judgment strives to do the right thing for the greatest number of people.

Mental Health/Elder Care Professionals. Having known many people with mental illness and lots of older people, I can tell you this is the new frontier. Maybe AI programs can help analyze a person, but they can't cure him or her. Therapy may be needed, which involves a very structured way of listening that fuses compassion, knowledge, and gut feelings. I'm not sure you could reliably program these human elements into a machine. One of my brothers is a substance abuse therapist, and he's good at it. Yet I know it took him years fighting his own struggles to attain the empathy he needed to do his job. Aging is another fusion of experience and knowledge. People can become cognitively impaired over time; their bodies break down. Some aspects of aging are poorly understood. Why do some people age gracefully and remain sharp into their nineties, while others suffer from dementia in their sixties? There are many mysteries yet to be unraveled. In a world in which everyone is aging, this is a universal problem that will demand multidisciplinary thinking. You'll not only need to understand medicine, psychology and sociology, you'll need to address humane ways of helping people when they become physically, mentally—and socially—disabled. It's one of the profoundly human challenges we face.[155]

3. **Acquire Basic Communication Skills.** I know a lot of people who *think* they can communicate. Then they start talking or writing. Or they get swamped in the mire of a slide presentation, usually freezing up when they have technical issues. In my travels and experiences (this is not a scientific observation), I've noticed most folks are awful to mediocre speakers, writers, and listeners. Throughout my career as a writer, speaker, and journalist, I've been honing my skills for more than 30 years. I've taken opportunities to improve myself at every level. I even earned a master's degree in communications, although it didn't prepare me for dealing directly with audiences. In order to be a fully enabled Quad I, you need to be able to communicate. That means conquering some fears. You may have the best ideas in the world for starting a new business, but if you can't communicate them, you're going to be unable to sell them to the world. That's why I recommend a boot camp approach to communication.

Questions to Ask:

A. Which are your strongest skills?

B. Which are your weakest skills?

C. Are you scared to death to speak in front of people?

D. How are your listening skills?

E. How would you gain more communications experience?

F. How can you write more and get it in front of people?

G. How can you overcome your fears of communicating?

H. Do you have a practice plan for regular speaking and writing?

BACKGROUNDER: 10 WAYS TO ACQUIRE COMMUNICATIONS SKILLS.

There are so many ways to gain the communications tools you need; the best news is that most of them are free. While I would certainly recommend you take adult-education, community, or four-year college courses in writing and speaking, the best approach is to engage your community. That means small, safe groups. Start slowly and work your way up. You don't have to envision yourself filling a stadium; a meeting at your home will be a great place to begin. Here are 10 suggestions to build your skill set:

Speak Locally. Every service club I know is constantly looking for speakers. Do you have a specialty or community service project? How about an interesting hobby or discovery? Have you taken an interesting trip lately that you'd like to share? Service clubs like the Kiwanis, Lions, Rotary, Exchange, et al., meet in nearly every town and have local chapters. They perform local service projects and raise money for things like college scholarships. Also consider your local chamber of commerce. Not only are you speaking—generally less than a half hour—you're networking as well. You may land a job offer. AI may be good at answering simple questions and ordering products, but it's not good at engaging audiences.

Join a Local Group. Again, the clubs I mentioned above are excellent places to start, but there are thousands of options. Public libraries sponsor writer's groups and hundreds of other hobby-oriented pursuits. You can tap your local park district, high school, or college for even more groups. Even houses of worship have their own specialty groups.

Joining usually means speaking—and often writing. That will get you engaged in communicating on an ever-larger scale.

Write a Blog or Newsletter. You want to start out by doing news items or updating people on a topic. For many people with ultra-specialized interests, that could lead to a significant audience. Are you interested in cooking, travel, or fossils? Write about it. Get it out to others. Worried about grammar and spelling? All word processing programs can help you out there. Keep in mind, though, that while some programs may do the writing for you, don't go the automation route. You'll need to write in your own voice, and don't worry if it's quirky. Be yourself.

Take an Online Course. Quite a few of them are free. Yet nearly every university offers them now, although they will charge tuition if you want college credit. If you don't have the time or flexibility to sit in a classroom, these are good venues. Just make sure that you have a chance to interact with a teacher. That's so you can get some feedback. You won't learn how to be a better writer unless someone is giving you constructive feedback.

Join an Incubator or Workspace. As noted earlier, these venues provide a social setting for you to learn about nearly every aspect of creating and running a venture. You can talk to experienced people whose knowledge ranges from marketing to finance. Many incubators will even have contests where you can design and pitch your business idea. The winners can reap venture capital to get their start-up off the ground. Some incubators even specialize in particular types of businesses such as fintech, foodtech, and healthtech. The best way to find and vet them is to do an online search of what you're looking for and what's available in your area. Although most of them charge membership fees, you may be able to walk around and hang out before you need to put your money down. Once you've found a comfortable space, you'll need to develop the communications skills you'll need to attract others to your ideas, build your business, and raise money. This is a total immersion environment, yet works if you're up to the challenge.

Bootstrap a Business. This is a smaller-scale approach than an incubator. Let's say you just want to start a small venture in your home. You don't have much money but have a lot of time. Where do you go? You'll need a *business plan*—how much money do you need, what do you plan to sell, and how do you plan to sell your product or service? Most community colleges provide business counselors and retired executives who can help you. While a much more streamlined model, *bootstrapping* still requires communications skills. You basically do everything yourself or with partners. You'll still need to write up your plan, present it, and try to convince others that it's worth investing in—even if you're just approaching your parents, friends, and neighbors for money.

Work for a Nonprofit. It doesn't matter if you're a Scout leader or trying to raise money for the charities. It all requires communication. You'll learn quite a bit working with others and be helping the community while doing it. It may lead to other things. You may connect with a network that can land you paid employment. I formed a nonprofit about a dozen years ago to address local property taxes, for example. We were extremely successful in raising awareness. We even wrote and passed a state law on taxes. And it led to my current vocation (I'm a county commissioner).

Pick a Cause and Show Up to Speak at Public Meetings. Every public body that I know of allows for public comment at the beginning or end of their meetings. Is there some local environmental cause you want to support? Do you oppose some proposed law or regulation? This is another opportunity to speak in public. You can give a brief statement in three minutes or less. It's a great way to enhance your speaking chops.

Write Online Articles. There are thousands of online publications that welcome nonprofessional writers who will contribute for free (not such as good thing for us professional scribes). You can pick any area of interest from computer games to New Zealand. If you go this route, make sure you are getting feedback from a professional editor, though. Many online sites just post without working with you to edit your work.

Become a Consummate Communicator. Although most people are reasonably good at one thing, strive to be a "three-tool player." That means being a competent writer, speaker, and *listener.* They all integrate: a good writer is a good listener (and reader). You should be able to ask and answer good questions. Audiences want interaction. They want you to engage with them. *Note: Reading from a piece of paper or slide deck isn't necessarily good communication.* The consummate communicator can do an entire talk without slides and dive into the audience for questions. And think of combing other talents to enrapture an audience. Are you a musician, storyteller, video producer, dancer, or artist? That gives you more arrows for your communications quiver. The bottom line: do everything you can do to connect with people on a human level.

Tell them your story and how you came to your subject. Backstories are important. Narrative details sew everything together. Listen to some of the storytelling programs on National Public Radio like *The Moth Radio Hour*. Learn how to tell a story, then learn how to grab an audience. It will take practice and courage, yet once you break through, you'll be able to sell yourself—and anything else you hope to do. In the thinking machine age, this will be a core skill of Quad I's.

4. **How to Organize Anything.** Machines can organize trillions of bytes of data. Yet they can't organize people. You may be thinking, *wait a minute, doesn't social media organize people?* I've heard this argument so many times, I roll my eyes when someone brings it up. Who organized the Arab Spring, yellow vest protests (in France), and climate change and women's marches around the world? Sure, social media posts get into people's heads, and there are millions of messages every day from hate forums to flash mobs. And everyone's doing it from a hacker in North Korea to a Russian troll. Yet you need to ask the question, if there are billions of messages in cyberspace—most people mostly ignore them—what gets them to actually *do something?* It's certainly not cute cat videos. Someone has to pick a time and place for them to show up and do something. Most of the time, they are benign events, although all too often they foment violence and terror. If you want to become a Quad I, you'll be able to organize not only yourself but others. This is truly a human skill. There is no one algorithm to make people take action or to show up in a room at a particular time. Trust me, as someone who's planned and organized hundreds of events, it's an art, not a science. Here's what you need to know:

Questions to Ask:

A. What do you want to organize?
B. Why do you want to organize an event or group?
C. What do you hope to accomplish?
D. How can others help you in organizing?
E. How can you motivate them to show up?
F. How can you publicize your event (e-mail, social media, flyers, etc.)?
G. What are your goals for organizing?
H. How does your organizing activity promote your integration and improvisation skills?

I.   What insights do you hope to gain?

J.   How many people do you hope to attract (high and low estimates)?

K.   Where can you learn organizing skills?

BACKGROUNDER: PICKING UP THE SKILLS YOU NEED TO ORGANIZE

As an organizer, I can tell you that there are no guarantees. You never know how many people are going to show up at your event. You never know how engaged they will be in your cause once they leave. Most of them will remain passive and do nothing. What if you succeed? Then you can build momentum for something bigger than yourself. It's extremely satisfying and can lead to other things. I started out small by organizing panels of journalists to speak at national conferences. I engaged journalists that I liked or knew to speak about things they cared about. Usually these were out-of-town conferences in New York City. I always followed up to ensure that they would show up on time and had some idea of the questions they would be asked. Then I graduated to organizing a local seminar that would involve booking a keynote speaker and panelists at a hotel. I organized several lecture series and eventually graduated to doing professional moderation and keynoting. Did I learn these skills in college? Even though I have a master's degree in communications (and a BA in psychology), I didn't take a single course in organizing. You can pick up these skills by volunteering for any local or trade organization. In my case, I was a persistent volunteer for my trade group (the Society of American Business Editors and Writers). I've also helped other groups find speakers and have a mental list of people I know could serve on panels or speak at conferences. Organizing melds many skills. You need to be able to communicate, motivate, and schedule people. You'll have to collaborate. If you're basically an introvert like me, it gets you out of your comfort zone, although once you master it, people will find their way to you. I've gained paid speaking engagements and article assignments through my organizing skills. It gets you in front of people and integrating with them. You'll expand your network and connect with people who can give you work. Whether you're trying to build a business or engage in your community, this is one skill that will open up doors. And it doesn't matter what subject you're organizing people to engage in; the sky's the limit. One guideline:

pick a passion and find like-minded people. It could be political or just raising money for a homeless shelter. Maybe you're doing a public information campaign on a health hazard or want to promote mountain biking. Whatever you do, it will extend your interests out into the world. Social media consumers can see a million messages a day, but it won't mean a thing to them 99 percent of the time. You're selling yourself and your ideas most of the time. If you can get others into a room to share thoughts—and their precious time—it's always a genuine accomplishment when there are so many other distractions.

5. **Learn to Go beyond the Data.** This is how we find *people* in a mass of numbers. As we detailed earlier in the book, machines are incredibly proficient at compiling and analyzing massive amounts of data. While on the surface we might think that companies like Amazon, Apple, and Facebook are friendly tech giants that want to make our lives better, think again. They are acquiring information about what we buy, consume, and prefer. They are getting this information so that they can precisely deliver advertising and sell us more of everything from books to thousand-dollar cellphones. I would wager that these companies know more about our habits, likes, and dislikes than *we* do. They are the corporate versions of Quad I's: they integrate all of this data into their business model because they can draw insights from the data they collect. While I'm not suggesting that you emulate what they do—you won't have the resources—you need to ask yourself some queries in this data-centric environment:

Questions to Ask:

A. Do you have some basic data analysis skills (spreadsheets, databases)?

B. How can you use those skills to mine data?

C. What would you like to know when mining data?

D. What big questions should we be asking big data (e.g., climate change, disease, water patterns)?

E. How can we use data to help people, possibly even predicting their behavior?

F. How can we identify harmful and violent behaviors through data?

G. How can we solve perennial problems through data analysis and knowledge of human conditions (e.g., crime, hunger, etc.).

BACKGROUNDER: FINDING THE HUMANITY IN BIG NUMBERS

I've always been fascinated with market manias and crashes. What makes people go loony and become obsessed with tulips, beanie babies, real estate, and stocks? What triggers those bubbles and what makes stocks crash? This is where data is showing you a picture, but not telling you the story. That's where a human narrative comes in. For example, on May 6, 2010, there was a "flash crash" that tanked markets around the world. A trillion dollars in market value evaporated in a matter of seconds. What triggered it? Did someone hack an exchange computer? Did algorithmic traders, that is, "robot traders," somehow go berserk? Nope. It was *one guy* in London. This rogue trader decided to submit $200 million worth of fake trades that were duplicated more than 19,000 times. The larger market, mostly guided by machines, read these faux trades as a sign that things were turning bearish. Since markets often ride on pure emotion, sell orders were automatically triggered and the market took a massive dive, later recovering. When the rogue trader was discovered, it raised some compelling questions about the *need* to go beyond the data: if humans are doing the programming, then they will build in often irrational human emotional triggers like fear and greed. "These algorithms weren't aware of the consequences of their decisions or the business context that drove their creation in the first place," write Nick Polson and James Scott in *AIG: How People and Machines Are Smarter Together*.[156] Remember, crunching and manipulating data is a powerful tool that you need to learn about. Just keep in mind that at the end of the analysis, there are people behind the programs. They may be hiding in plain sight and are often the ghosts in the machine.

6. **Find Flow.** There are many names for optimal experience: getting a rush, a natural high, a stream of consciousness. The psychologist Mihaly Csikszentmihalyi called it "flow" and believed it was the best part of being human. It comes from both mastering something and doing it as well as you can. It occupies your entire being. It's the time when you feel most alive. All pain disappears and you're able to transcend yourself. Maybe you're a figure skater and you do a triple axel or a chess player and you conquer a much better player. You can see well beyond your own mind and body at that point. It's like floating in a space of your own. That's the state of flow. "They are situations in which attention can be freely invested to achieve a person's goals, because there is no disorder to straighten out, no threat for the self to defend against . . . and those who attain it [flow] develop a more stronger, more confident

self because more of their psychic energy has been invested success-fully in goals they themselves had chosen to pursue," writes Csikszent-mihalyi.[157] Why is a flow state important? While they can master many things, it's hard to say whether machines will ever feel great doing something. When we feel enlivened about something, we're creative and powerful. We can think in ways we never imagined. We can write bet-ter books or draw better pictures. The world becomes clearer. We can be our better selves. How do we get there?

Questions to Ask:

A. What kinds of things do you do to achieve an optimal experience (we're not talking about sex, drugs, and rock 'n' roll, by the way)?

B. How do you find "self-conscious assurance"? This is where the mind and soul take over and leave the ego behind.

C. How do you focus your attention on the task and leave the world behind? This might involve prayer, meditation, yoga, or centering your mind.

D. How do you discover new solutions? Being a good problem solver can put you in a flow state. I love it when I can find simple solutions and fix things.

E. How do you become an "autotelic self"? This is the kind of person who relishes challenges because they can stick to—and achieve—their goals.

F. How do you pay attention and be present? Sometimes you have to be absolutely in the moment to see what's going on or a potential solution. That means getting away from your devices and focusing on one per-son of activity. You also need to be able to enjoy the present.

BACKGROUNDER: BUILDING A FLOW EXPERIENCE

There are people who relish busy places and those who can't stand crowds. I'm kind of an oddball. I feel right at home in the middle of New York City and can't wait to enter the sanctum of a library reading room. I can find quiet in both places. The key in both places is the ability to quiet your mind and body. While I find it useful to tell people about meditation, I've never been able to do it myself. Maybe I've never practiced it enough. Instead I do *Qi Gong*, which is a Chinese energy exercise, regular aerobic exercise (bike riding), and lots of walking—three times a day. A decent walk or bike ride almost always does the trick. Sometimes I get into a flow state doing these activities, especially when I work up a rhythm. Then again, thoughts start flowing when I stop thinking about all the things I have to do and I let my mind wander. Then improvisation kicks in, and I don't have to directly think about a problem. Ideas emerge. Then I can write whole paragraphs and outline entire chapters—in my head. Needless to say I've practiced this over decades. Yet every time it happens, I'm kind of amazed, because I know anyone can do it. Whether you're trying to solve a math problem, write a program, create a sculpture, or tackle climate change, you'll need to immerse yourself in something you've mastered. There are lot of physicists who are excellent classical musicians. Some doctors are great tennis players. It's mastery that counts. You don't have to be a pro, but you should get to the point where whatever you're doing makes you feel vibrantly immortal. One other thing that makes us human in this journey: if you're able to find that quiet place, you may even have a deeply spiritual experience. "When you've been able to still all the noise inside of you, when you've been able to establish silence, you begin to hear the deepest kind of calling from within yourself," finds Thich Nhat Hanh, the Buddhist monk and teacher. Maybe flow won't help you find a revelation, but it may keep you on the road to discovery.

7. **Find an Open-minded Environment.** One of the worst things I hear all the time is "this is the way we've always done it." I don't mind tradition at all. In some situations, it's really grounding. Yet it can be stifling, especially in the thinking machine age. You can't find new ideas in a place where philosophy and free expression are stifled in any way. No one group has an exclusive license on the truth, technology, or new ways of thinking. Creativity and ideas will come from places that you least suspect. Isaac Newton was said to be under an apple tree when he came up with his world-changing ideas on gravity (the descendent of "the tree" is supposedly at Trinity College, Cambridge). Was Newton at Cambridge when he came up with his theories and extraordinary equations? Nope. He was out in the country avoiding a plague that was ravaging English cities at the time. So finding the ideas you need to succeed is often a matter of *where* you are. If you're surrounded by like-minded people or in a stifling setting, you might not get bonked by the proverbial apple. There may be no apples around. You'll need to know the following:

Questions to Ask:

A. Do you need to move to another city?

B. What cities promote creativity, learning, and start-ups?

C. What cities or areas favor "cultural creatives"?

D. Will you need more education if you need to relocate?

E. How would you support yourself if you need to move?

F. Would you need several jobs to survive in your new locale?

G. Could you count on any financial support if you move (help from parents, scholarships)?

BACKGROUNDER: PLACES THAT PROMOTE CREATIVITY

Where you go depends on what you want to do. Some cities are tech hubs (Boston, New York, San Francisco), while others may promote a diversified economy (Chicago, Columbus, Nashville). There is no list of the perfect place to go. You may want to combine a relocation with education. If that's your mission, then nearly any college town is a good place to start, although the top three tech cities are challenging because of the cost of living. Yet there are plenty of bargain-priced cities from Gainesville to Kansas City, where you can find the arts and thriving creative scene.

If you want to go overseas, you could live much cheaper while experiencing emerging economies. The United Nations (UNESCO) maintains a "Creative Cities Network" of places on nearly every continent that promote art, design, film, literature, media, and music.[158] If you're looking to relocate, consider cities that offer a sweet spot between cultural (the arts, design, music, museums) and economic capital (venture capital, angel investors, banks). If you want to study and pursue a design career, it helps to be in cities where that thrives (Brooklyn, Tokyo) You can pursue a career nearly anywhere, although it always helps to be near major research institutions like land-grant colleges or even smaller liberal arts schools. Diversity is also important, so you may consider cities that are typically not on anybody's radar such as Detroit, Akron, and Minneapolis.

You need to find a culture that is a best fit for what you want to do in a place that you can afford. "Culture, then," writes urbanologist Richard Florida, "is bound up with the New Urban Crisis—a crisis of development and success—which is making our largest and most dynamic cities more expensive and less affordable, and in doing so, threatens the very economic, racial, and cultural diversity which has fueled their cultural creativity in the first place."[159]

Most importantly, you'll need to find a place that promotes innovation and a free exchange of ideas. We often learn the most from people who are nothing like us (that's where diversity comes in). But these folks should feel like they can share their ideas without any repression. Joe Davis, chief economist for the Vanguard Group, which manages trillions of dollars, calls these environments "idea multipliers." They range from Renaissance Italy to Silicon Valley. The most creative people tend to gravitate to places where they can promote often-crazy ideas like the computer mouse or a phone that's as powerful as a laptop. Ideas lead to patents and patents lead to profitable products. You need to be in the room where these things happen, even if they have nothing to do with technology. "The globalization we should care about increasingly in a knowledge-based economy is the trade of ideas," Davis says, "not the trade of commodities. Although the rise of tariffs is concerning, this force is 10 times more powerful than the trade of commodities."[160] In a globalized world, this mindset translates into being open to ideas from China, India, and other developing countries. You won't get the full picture until you have some perspective of what other cultures and countries are doing. Since the world's population will always need food, clean water, medicine, and ways to deal with aging, these are common research subjects. We will need new agricultural methods, materials, and technologies for solutions to climate change and migrating populations. Look abroad for inspiration. "There's 10 times more powerful trade in ideas and knowledge than commodities," Davis notes.[161]

8. **Give Yourself a Financial Cushion.** No matter where you go or what you do, unless your family is subsidizing your journey, you'll need to pay your own way. Although personal finance education has improved in recent years, it's never been great in the United States. We have millions of messages telling us to buy something every moment of the day and far too few telling us to save. Even when "big savings" are advertised, merchants are really telling us to *buy*. This culture is hard to resist, especially when you're online. While shopping malls and most conventional retail outlets are struggling, it's much more efficient to shop on the Internet. Not only is it more efficient, advertisers seem to know exactly what you've bought and what you're likely to buy, so pop-up screen ads entice you even more. That's because specialized algorithms, based on your social media and search engine requests, are monitoring your online activity for clues on your overall consumption. Have you ever clicked on that hip hoodie or bought a streaming video or tune? Online merchants know and see all. But all of this consumption can get you into debt. Yet you'll need to be able to save money if you're to prosper. This is not something being broadcast on any cable channel or portal. You just have to do it. Savings will cushion the blow if you

lose or quit a job or experience setbacks. It also helps if you have health insurance. Here's what you need to know:

Questions to Ask:

A. How much can you save every month?

B. Are you "paying yourself first" by saving something before paying bills?

C. If employed, are you automatically saving part of your salary through a 401(k), 403(b), or 457 plan?

D. If not, how much can you contribute? (at least 15 percent of your annual salary is good).

E. If your employer doesn't offer a retirement plan, have you set up an Individual Retirement Account (IRA) or ROTH IRA (I suggest both)?

F. Do you have a rainy-day fund for emergencies (it should be roughly one-third of your take-home pay) in cash (money-market or checking accounts)?

G. Do you have health insurance on your own, through school or parents? You can always buy a bare-bones "catastrophic" policy that will cover extreme medical expenses. Google "Affordable Care Act policies" for your state.

H. Are you avoiding debt at all costs? I recommend paying off your credit cards every month and completely avoiding payday, pawn shop, and vehicle title loans (the finance charges are obscene!)

I. If you have debts, do you have a plan to pay them off? Keep in mind that debts such as student loans will hold you back from buying cars, homes, and furthering your education.

J. Do you employ compound interest? This simple math multiplies your money. A $1,000 account invested at 5 percent annual interest with $100 monthly contributions amounts to $88,000 over 30 years.[162] Think of what you could do with larger amounts of money.

K. Do you have a financial plan? In general terms, when would you like to retire and how much would it cost?

L. What are your most important savings goals (e.g., college, vehicles, a car, vacations, more education)?

M. How much will you need to save to achieve your goals? Do the math. There are lots of online calculators.

BACKGROUNDER: BUILDING THAT CUSHION

I'll keep this simple. The best way to protect against emergencies and achieve your long-term goals is to create three buckets:

- **Short-Term Bills (bucket #1).** These are monthly expenses, which include paying off your credit card, rent/mortgage, food, transportation, and discretionary expenses (restaurants, drinks, entertainment). If you're not making enough to cover these monthly expenses, then don't go into debt. You'll need to be frugal and reserve for emergencies.

- **Mid-Term Bills.** If your employer isn't withholding income taxes (and you're self-employed), you'll need to estimate and pay quarterly taxes. You also may have to reserve money for bills coming due like insurance and property taxes. You can also put education savings (graduate or certificate training) in this bucket—if it's several years away.

- **Long-Term Bills.** This is mostly retirement and big goals like buying a home (or second home). As with the other two buckets, you need to be saving for these goals on a monthly basis. Only check this bucket once a year, but keep those automatic payments coming!

How best to achieve your savings goals? Again, make it automatic and simple. You can ask a bank or mutual fund company to withdraw money from your checking account every month. What you can't touch, you probably won't spend. If saving for the long-term bucket, set up a portfolio of stock and bond mutual funds through your employer-sponsored plan. And if you're self-employed, you can set you your own SEP-IRA or Self-401(k). Any mutual fund company can help you do this, or you can go to a robo adviser and set it up on your mobile device. Since I've been writing about saving and investing for decades, I can tell you that it's gotten so easy to save you can do it on your phone. We're in the midst of a techno-savings revolution and it's only going to get better, so avail yourself of all of the tools that are accessible. They're even pleasant to use.

9. **How to Find Meaning and the Right Attitude.** Now it's time to get into the soil of mortality. This is your big picture, and it may be a bit fuzzy. Yet how you view yourself and your future will make a colossal difference in the world of automation. The point of this exercise is to figure out what's important to you. While you can certainly pick up a lot in school, for most people, it's not enough. You'll certainly need to wander out into the world, have some new experiences, and see what works for you. There will be more misses than hits—and that's okay. For some people, it's becoming a special education teacher, while others

are perfectly okay being a first responder. I've grown up with people who had careers in accountancy; consulting; electrical, chemical and nuclear engineering; language translation; lawyering; doctoring; and quite a few artists. By the way, you can still be active in the arts while holding onto a profession to pay the bills. Nearly all of the lawyers I know are published authors. I'm a writer and a performing musician, in addition to a few other things. However you define yourself, find things that provide meaning. I love performing now because I love to see kids dancing. I didn't always feel that way since I was a classically trained violinist and was estranged from music for decades. At the very least, your passions and purpose will buoy you in the coming massive wave of automation. What do you need to know to find meaning?

Questions to Ask:

A. What kind of music, art, or literature stays with you?

B. What have you read that you can't get out of your head and speaks to you?

C. What do you do that makes you feel like you're making a contribution to society and your community?

D. If you were to study something or do an activity, what would it be?

E. Where would you have to go to find meaning?

F. How do you define yourself now? Use a word to describe who you are.

G. How would you like to describe yourself?

H. If you only had a month to live, what would you do and want to leave behind?

I. If you only had a year to live, what would you want to do?

J. What would you like your most important contribution or epitaph to be? Ponder Thomas Jefferson's gravestone ("Author of the Declaration of Independence [and] of the Statute of Virginia for religious freedom & Father of the University of Virginia"). I know, that's not fair. Just think of one great thing you want to leave behind.

BACKGROUNDER: SPECIFIC PLACES TO FIND MEANING

Without question, unless you're a saint or a mystic, most likely it will take a variety of experiences to tell you what's meaningful. I can tell you what's meaningful to me, but it probably won't work for you. There's no algorithm that can program meaning. You have to find it for yourself. The process is called being human. You can transact your being by experiencing, learning, and doing. For those who love books, there's an awful lot to mine in great novels and classic works. You may have a band that you could see a hundred times and not get tired of their repertoire. A sport may provide some incentive for you to get out and better yourself. Or you may find the answer to life just being quiet and meditating. Since we're individuals, we can customize everything. Of course, there's an art to the search for meaning, just as there's an art to life itself. Do what the machines can't do— live the life you want. Here are some guidelines that I've found useful:

- **Tinker Around.** As I noted in an earlier chapter, my dad had a workshop. Once I knew what every tool could do, I started to play around with my own ideas. Whether it was building a Pinewood Derby car for Scouts or a spaceship that would never fly, I let my imagination run wild—and tried to build things that I saw in my mind. It didn't matter to me if I didn't get a job at NASA. I was on a journey in my basement. It's okay to tinker your entire life. I have. You never know what you'll come up with. Things like batteries, steel plows, barbed wire, electric lights, paper, and wheels have come from small workshops. And boy did these inventions have meaning: seemingly little objects that changed our lives in profound ways. "Inventions shape our lives in unpredictable ways—and while they're solving a problem for someone, they're often causing a problem for someone else," writes Tim Harford in *Fifty Inventions That Shaped the Modern Economy*.[163] Without a doubt, a little imagination in a small space can make a big difference on so many levels.

- **Explore and Address a Local Problem.** This is where change begins. It doesn't matter where you start. You could be protesting a local dump issue or a bigger problem like homelessness. Maybe you volunteer at a food pantry. Helping others is almost always meaningful. It gets you out of your head and your own personal bubble. You see needs. Maybe you will think of better ways of addressing them. You start small on a human scale one on one, then see the bigger picture. "To make a sustainable city," writes Wendell Berry, "one must begin somehow and I think the beginning must be small and economic."[164]

- **Explore Your Sensitivities.** Being human means that certain things in life impact you more than others. I have a pachyderm skin for criticism—I've been a journalist for more than 40 years—but others crumble when they get the stink eye from anyone. I'm not being judgmental, but you need to explore what provokes a reaction. A lot of us avoid certain situations like door-knocking and asking for money, while others are seemingly born into sales and marketing. Are you an introvert (inward-seeking) or extrovert (outward)? Knowing yourself will help you find meaning in a world of noise. As Susan Cain writes in *Quiet*, a classic study on introverts. "Many psychologists agree that introverts and extroverts work differently. Extroverts tend to tackle assignments quickly. They make fast (sometimes rash) decisions and are comfortable multi-tasking and risk taking. . . . Introverts often work more slowly and deliberately. They like to focus on one task at a time and can have mighty powers of concentration."[165] Stop and take a few moments to ask yourself who you are and how you react to different situations. You may have to slow down and turn off your devices for a while.

- **How Can You Fill Your Life with Meaning?** I've always found meaning in arts, books, music, and great lives. I can relish a good biography the way some folks enjoy a glass of wine or a meal. Of course, there's much to be absorbed from reading great books, and you don't have to feel bad if you haven't read but a handful of them. Some books—Kant's *Critique of Pure Reason* and Twain's *Huckleberry Finn* come to mind— may torment you for a long time, while others are a pure delight. Pick a subject you're passionate about. Do you like science? What about ancient philosophy? Or maybe you just want to make a quilt. It doesn't matter. There is no right approach or perfect book or activity list. I would keep a journal of books or activities that you like and dislike. If you want to tackle a list of classics, you could pick up Susan Wise Bauer's *The Well-Educated Mind*. I've worked through some gems, but I have a long way to go. The main purpose of this exercise is to find ideas that are important to you and continue your inquiry. "Classical self-education demands that you understand, evaluate and react to ideas," Bauer suggests.[166] Anybody can do this. It will take a lifetime and you'll never be finished.

- **Seek Wisdom.** I know we're really getting into the weeds, but this is maybe the most important part of this exercise. You can't find meaning without self-knowledge and wisdom. I can't tell you where it is, because you'll have to find it yourself in any number of places. I've always admired the life of Michel de Montaigne, the man who pretty much invented the personal essay in Shakespeare's time. His essays are remarkable works of reflection, insight, humor, and observation. They are also loaded with wisdom. You can go back to them and read between the lines. Montaigne had been a wealthy public servant and diplomat, then literally retreated to a tower on his estate in southern France to write some of the most sparkling prose ever. How did he find wisdom? He had been in society as mayor of his town (Bordeaux). He traveled and tried to avoid the horrible religious wars at the time while making friends and eating, drinking, and living well. And there was one essential thing that he did that helped him observe his own life: he spent long stretches doing nothing except for reading, walking, and sleeping. Montaigne's unoccupied mind freed him for his luminous writing. "Just as the tiger stripes of life lurch about, so an unoccupied mind gyrates unpredictably and brings forth mad, directionless whimsies," writes Sarah Bakewell in her glorious *How to Live or a Life of Montaigne*. This isn't to say that Montaigne was mentally ill. *Au contraire.* The clarity and honesty of his prose is timeless. He lived a great life and wanted to share it with us. You know how hard that is (then and now)? We still enjoy his thoughts nearly five centuries after he first penned them. I can't tell you where to find wisdom, but I will tell you it's all around you. Go talk to a veteran or your grandparents. Spend some time with your teachers after class. Wander over to the nearest union hall or hospital. Wherever people are engaged with life at the loudest volumes, that's where you'll find wisdom. Yet don't be afraid to ask questions. It won't magically come out of your smart speaker or phone. It's not in a gaming program and is certainly never going to be streaming at you. Seeking isn't necessary *finding*, but keep on asking. It may take a while for even little bits of wisdom to add up to meaning in your life. The right attitude is more a state of mind, and it sounds really corny: *always* search for wisdom, those kernels that are going to get your through the days of your life. It's like panning for gold, but it's also a lot of fun. Then you can answer the question "what the heck am I doing in my life." That's rough going for most folks. Time to hit the hills.

10. **Focus on the Infinite.** Yikes. This doesn't make sense, does it? Isn't this an oxymoron? How could you possibly focus on something that big and gnarly? Well, let's reverse engineer this a bit. Most people are incredibly unfocused unless they're pursuing something like a degree or working on a project. Even then, it's easy to get distracted. You pick up your smartphone or check your e-mail. The TV or radio in on. *We're*

on all the time. I'm sure I'm fudgy on the science, but there's a reason why people have attention deficit disorders. There's too much coming at us, and it's hard to turn off. Some of us may even be addicted to gaming, streaming and constant stimulation. Our brains are hardwired for this brain candy. This exercise is to take a vast pool of ideas and narrow them down into digestible and meaningful bites (or bytes). This will help you prioritize what you need to do:

Questions to Ask:

A. What five things do you hope to accomplish?
B. Of those five things, can you narrow them down to the top three?
C. What would be on the top of your list?
D. What would you need to succeed in achieving your prime items?
E. Would you need to involve other people? Who would they be?
F. Would you need to organize a group to accomplish your goals?
G. Once you had your group together, how would you keep things on course?
H. What would you need to do to keep yourself and your group motivated and focused?

BACKGROUNDER: WAYS OF ACQUIRING AND MAINTAINING FOCUS

Whatever you choose to do, not only do you need to set some goals, you'll need a reliable rudder to keep you on course. I've seen so many people that have gotten distracted that they've lost their way. I've been, of course, a few times myself. The job market hands you some detours. You lost a position after building a new home. Kids come along and you need to clothe, feed, and educate them. Relatives are diagnosed with cancer. You have to tend to your parents when they become invalid. I wouldn't call these distractions; it's just life. They are events and situations that you have no control over, but if you're a responsible addict you have to deal with them. How do you stay focused in the midst of the utter chaos of living a life? You'll need some structure for one thing. Then you'll need a rubric for dealing with those squalls that rip at your mainsail. Here's some guidance:

• **Meaning Is Your Mode for Discovery.** Stop crowding your life with meaningless activities. Only you know what they are, and you could be wasting money and time on them in any number of ways. I used to savor the idea of going out to eat, for example. At the places I went to, though, the quality of the food never got any better. You'd pay as much for a glass of wine as you would for an entire *bottle* at the supermarket. And the money we spent was meaningless, unless it was for a special occasion like a birthday. My wife and I could make much better steaks at home. Then we had to ask ourselves: what was meaningful about dining out? Well, very little, other than the need to get out of the house. So we substituted just sitting in a coffee shop and talking instead of spending hundreds of dollars on mediocre meals. What we really found meaning in was being present and talking to each other, listening carefully in a quiet environment. Where do you find meaning? Some find it in rituals, particularly religious ones. I still like going to ballparks like Wrigley Field. Others may find it in gardening or taking a car ride across the country. Camping and exploring can be fun. Pick your own pursuits. If you find meaning in something, it will definitely help you focus and screen activities that are mere distractions. That's going to be essential in your work life. "Once an individual's search for meaning is successful," writes Viktor Frankl in his classic *Man's Search for Meaning*, it not only renders him [or her/they] happy, but also gives him the capability to cope with suffering."[167]

- **Make Focused Attention the Driver of Excellence.** You may already have some great ideas for a career or business. They just need to be pulled together and fine-tuned. That requires adjusting the lens on what you're doing. You'll need what psychologist Daniel Goleman calls "focused attention." This is the ability to lock in on a specific task or project and screen out all other distractions. Most people can do this, but they have to practice it. Athletes have spent thousands of hours training to do focused attention to improve performance, as have musicians, chess players, and anyone who needs to concentrate for a specific period of time. For a great example, watch any Grand Slam tennis match. The players are not thinking about the entire match; they are playing one point at a time. They are trying to anticipate top spin, hitting solid backhands, and acing their serves. When they give up a point, or make a forced error, they try to maintain their focus for the next serve or volley. Focused attention helps them keep their heads in the game— and get better. The brain is building itself up during this process and we're able to master something over time. "We learn best with focused attention," Goleman found. "As we focus on what we're learning, our brain maps that information on what we already know, making new neural connections."[168]

- **Channel Your Emotions to Maintain Focus.** I can't tell you how many times I've seen people "lose it" in public. They put on an emotional display that's so strident that whatever they wanted to say was diluted by their outburst. We see it from children all the time, but some people never seem to grow up. Self-control plays a big part in focusing on your message and goals. Yet emotion shouldn't be entirely left out of the equation. We will need a full range of feelings to achieve what we need. For example, how could a social worker friend I know function and find meaning in her job without genuine compassion? It's part of the makeup of being a human service professional. In nearly all lines of work, we often see people at their worst, and it's impossible not to have an emotional reaction. What we can fall back on is a rubric that emotions are the fabric of our being, although what stitches us together is a focus on who we are and what we hope to achieve. We can still experience everything we need to—joy, hatred, grief, pride. The key to maintaining focus is to not let those emotions take over. Letting them become a dominant part of the narrative leads to hate crimes, murder, and fascism. How do we suppress the dark angels of our nature? By acknowledging them and keeping them in their place. Know that they are part of behavioral and complex social systems. "Problems of such complexity and urgency require an approach to problem-solving that integrates our self-awareness and how we act, and our empathy and compassion, with a nuanced understanding of the systems at play," Goleman adds.[169] Or we could start with Polonius's advice to Laertes in *Hamlet*, in which he advises his son on self-restraint and "to thine own self be true."

- **Adopt Project-Based Thinking.** Was Michelangelo thinking about sculpting while he was painting the ceiling of the Sistine Chapel? I don't know, although I know his powers of concentration allowed him to finish most of his masterpieces. While I admire Leonardo da Vinci, in contrast, there are a lot of projects he didn't finish. He designed a mammoth equestrian statue, for example, although maybe the casting technology at the time just couldn't execute his vision. Having a deadline for anything gives you fairly solid focus. As a journalist and writer— even as a speaker—your time on any project (except for the Great

American Novel) is always limited. Some of the most scattered folks I know never really abide by deadlines. Everything is in their head, and they just can't complete anything. In any project, focus on what you can accomplish with stages. I always start out with a pro forma outline. This is a fuzzy picture of what should be in every chapter. Then I flesh it out. From there, I estimate the time it would take to research, write, and edit every chapter up until the time I submit it to a publisher. That doesn't end the process, though. I will receive edits and revisions back from my editor, then corrections from the copy editor. I will read proofs of the pages at least three times before it goes to press. Then I will have to promote and speak about the book, so I have to plan out another few months. I counseled a few authors on how to do this; I suspect that many aspiring writers like the idea of writing and publishing a book, yet don't think in terms of the project and the time commitment. It's a process that requires a fair amount of careful planning. Only geniuses can stare at a blank page every day and come up with something brilliant without this structure (although I would surmise that they always have an outline of sorts).

- **Use Powerful Tools to Keep Focused.** I'm always amazed at how little confidence people have in trying new things. They tell me "I can never do that!" when I know they've never tried. Maybe they've been told as children to be limited; sometimes they've been abused. You'll face some powerful obstacles in the workplace of the future. The biggest roadblock will be yourself. There's a way around the boulders you put in your own path. According to Goleman, Paul Kaufman, and Michael Ray in their delightful book *Creative Spirit*, you can harness your inner toolbox by having faith in own creativity, getting rid of judgment, making precise observations, and asking penetrating questions. In practical terms, this translates to "seeing the world with a wonder of a child and the precision of a scientist. It means engaging everything around you with a refreshed awareness."[170] How do you engage these tools? Listen. Be playful. Doodle. Go to museums. Take a long walk in a park or forest preserve. Journal. Sketch. Photograph. Record. Most of these tools are immediately accessible and don't require upgrades or batteries. They are really cheap and you can get them just about anywhere. Just be open to possibilities. You don't have to be an *artiste* to do art. You're an explorer now. Vanquish those negative thoughts or you'll never take the first step.

- **Find Balance and Live Deeply.** What gives focus to our lives even when we're deeply concentrating on getting a better job or completing dream goals? It's not doing too much. I love writing and interacting with people, but I know I need solitude. I need breaks and naps or my back and butt get sore. I need to step away from the outside world and cyber media on a regular basis. I strive to find balance. You'll need what Joel and Michelle Levey call "compassionate awareness." This is a holistic way of smoothing out your life. I'm sure you know when you're working, eating, drinking, or slumming too much. You need to be honest with yourself. You'll also need a sense of when you're overspending or not spending enough time on minding your career or family concerns. Self-honesty is always a tiny cat that is mewing in the alley. Compassionate awareness is about caring for yourself and others. In addition to all of the other advice in this section, if you practice this form of self-preservation, you may even manage to live a deep and meaningful life. Yet you'll have to focus on the parts of your life that often get neglected. In Western society, we're overstressed, so we often burn out before we realize what's happening. Paying attention to—and practicing—stress management by having a proper, balanced diet, exercise, and rest is key to maintaining focus on a holistic lifestyle, the Leveys advise.[171] You'll also need to quiet down and find a serene place, whether it's in your mind or a physical location. "Learning to quiet one's body and mind, and to raise or deepen the quality of our mindful awareness, is the essential first step toward living in balance, realizing optimal health, and gaining guiding insights that nourish our lives with inspiration and meaning," the Leveys observe.[172]

- **Maintain a Spiritual Lens.** This exercise doesn't necessarily involve a specific religion, but if you have a faith tradition that gives you a harmonic center, embrace it. By spiritual, I mean seeing the divine or sacred in all things: in nature, in inanimate objects, and in other people. Believe me, there are saints among us, even though they haven't been canonized by any church. Just walk into any hospital or senior care facility, firehouse or police station and you'll find plenty of people with halos. You just need to look carefully. Focusing on the sacred and divine is hard to do when we're overwhelmed by an endless stream of images and sound. The world is brimming with sensations that are hurting our spirit. In order to gain focus on what's important, you'll need to hear your inner voice and listen to others. I've found divinity in music and singing. When I hear Beethoven's Ninth Symphony, I usually tear up. I have the same reaction to Bach. Something stirs me. I'm moved by great paintings and literature. The last line of Fitzgerald's *Great Gatsby* still dries up my throat. And there's something about plays like *Death of a Salesman* and *Romeo and Juliet* that tears at me. Those narratives never go away and are spiritual experiences for me. Art helps me focus on my work and get through some challenging days. Songs will fly into my head even if I'm not listening to a device. I'll hear Springsteen or Hank Williams while riding my bike. I'll take a walk and hear Mozart. It's like I don't even need to ever hear those recordings again. I can even write whole paragraphs or songs in my head even though I'm nowhere near a computer or instrument. Perhaps my tunes and words will fade into the fog of mortality, and that will be painful to me. But I will keep on focusing the lens I have until I can't see. It's what a need to do. It's what we all need to do. "Each of us can open our eyes wide and meet the world with courage," suggests *Living Deeply*, a book from the Institute of Noetic Sciences. "If your mind is open, your attention trained, your perception clear and broad and your intention pure and strong, you can follow the flashes of inspiration that appear to you every day."[173] Focus on the signs around you that tell you where you are, who you are, and where you can go. If you're paying close enough attention, even the most automated world will have a distinct and wonderful place for you.

Postscript

GOING OVER TO THE DARK SIDE: ABOUT AI AND THE SINGULARITY

Let's say you've accepted the bright side of this book's premise that you can work alongside machines with your enhanced human skills and prosper. Now let's venture over to the dark side. What if we create a global network of artificial intelligence that decides that it can run the show better than we can? That's not much of a stretch given any day's headlines, but now we need to dance over into the realm of speculation.

Now we've ventured into what scientist Ray Kurzweil calls the "singularity."[174] That's the point at which artificial intelligence has reached the level of human intelligence—and there's no turning back. Kurzweil, a multitalented inventor, is the director of engineering at Google as I write this. He's been focused on his singularity prediction for many years; it's 2045 by his most recent estimate.

To understand what Kurzweil means by the singularity, you need to know what happens first. He surmises that a computer will be able to pass a Turing test by 2029. This is a benchmark when we can't tell the difference between a computer's response to a set of hard questions and that of a human. The test was named after Alan Turing, a computer scientist genius who pioneered programmable computers during World War II to break the Germans' devilish enigma code. Although Turing's computers helped the Allies win the war, he was later arrested for being gay and persecuted, losing his security clearance. He committed suicide by swallowing cyanide in 1954. (He's portrayed by Benedict Cumberbatch in the movie *The Imitation Game*).[175]

A computer passing the Turing test will supposedly be able to distinguish between "being catty" (elusive) and acting like a feline, among other things.

What happens when machines get to that level of intelligence? Kurzweil predicts that then we can integrate thinking machines into our own brains and vice versa. Machine learning and memory can then directly replace or augment human capabilities in a chimeric union. Imagine being able to insert a microchip in the brain of someone suffering from Alzheimer's disease to restore their memory or to insert code into someone's lung to vanquish a tumor?

"Ultimately, it will affect everything," Kurzweil says optimistically of the singularity. "We're going to be able to meet the physical needs of all humans. We're going to expand our minds and exemplify these artistic qualities that we value."[176]

But what about the machine takeover part? If machines can think for themselves, why would they mess around with *us* being their masters? Wouldn't they look at our violence, greed, self-obsession, and vanity and change things around? Wouldn't the master become the slave?

Kurzweil remains optimistic that the machines won't bother with total human domination. He's bright-eyed about the singularity's potential good deeds. In his view, we're most of the way there to better living through machine thinking.

"What's actually happening is machines are powering all of us," Kurzweil said. "They're making us smarter. They may not yet be inside our bodies—but by the 2030s we will connect our neo-cortex, the part of our brain where we do our thinking, to the cloud.[177]

"We're going to get more neo-cortex, we're going to be funnier, we're going to be better at music, we're going to be sexier. We're really going to exemplify all the things that we value in humans to a greater degree," he said.[178]

Maybe Kurzweil underestimates the degree to which machines will occupy our psyches. Why would machines stop at making *individuals* better people? What if they started to reengineer entire global *systems* like banking, markets, and power distribution? Why stop at making people funnier and better musicians? If I was chief technologist of the world, I'd want to work to eliminate global poverty, find freshwater and food for everyone, and prevent global market crashes and depressions. I'd want to halt wars over natural resources that have been the source of far too many conflicts and engineer a smart solution for climate change that doesn't further damage the planet (I think we have some good ideas on that already without computer assistance). I'd also want to engineer a political solution to the massive economic inequality we see that leaves tens of millions of people without toilets while a handful of billionaires can own entire islands and entire fleets of boats and jets (and gold toilets). That would be my machine optimism.

THE DARK SIDE ILLUMINATED

Getting the global economic and political system hardwired into digital control is not that far-fetched, and it was contemplated long before Kurzweil conceived of his singularity.

Isaac Asimov, in "I, Robot," lays out a different scenario that's more akin to Hollywood's prevailing view. Originally published as a series of short stories beginning in 1940, "I, Robot" has become the inspiration for hundreds of other stories and films. Despite its dark ending (read on), his book starts out with a simple premise: that all robots should follow a set of rigid rules:

Isaac Asimov's Three Laws of Robotics

1. A robot may not injure a human being, or, through inaction, allow a human being to come to harm.
2. A robot must obey the orders given to it by human beings except where such orders would conflict with the First Law.
3. A robot must protect its own existence as long as such protection does not conflict with the First or Second Law.[179]

As you know from viewing most any film involving robots, machines can be really mean, coming to believe that rules are made to be broken. Once they get up a head of steam (or advanced neural network functioning), they can lay waste to humanity and entire planets. The Martian robots were especially nasty.

Was Asimov thinking about getting his provocative stories on screen when he created his robot world right at the beginning of World War II? I'm sure he was interested in that route—it took some 70 years for a decent Hollywood version of "I, Robot" to emerge—but he had his eye on what robots would ultimately do if they had the chance. Here's one of the closing paragraphs of the last story. The main characters are talking about a world run by machines:

> "But are you telling me, Susan [the scientist/protagonist], that the 'Society for Humanity' is right; that Mankind *has* lost its way?"

"It never had any, really. It was always at the mercy of economic and sociological forces it did not understand—at the whims of climate, and the fortunes of war. Now the Machines understand them; and no one can stop them, since the Machines will deal with them as they are dealing with The Society—having, as they do, the greatest of weapons at their disposal, the absolute control of our economy."[180]

I felt chills when Asimov mentioned climate and "control of the economy." I'm not sure, but I wonder if he was pondering global warming. He certainly would've had access to current research. He had a PhD in chemistry from Columbia University. Scientists have known about global warming since the 1890s; global temperatures have been on the rise since the beginning of the Industrial Revolution.

On the economic reference, there's a more compelling insight to examine. In ways that are not even being discussed, an enormous volume (trillions of dollars) of our money transactions have gone digital. Banks routinely wire money between themselves and customers. You can send a payment via your phone to nearly anyone. You can even keep your retirement portfolio online. You could accumulate hundreds of millions of dollars and not see a single bit of paper currency. Hackers are constantly trying to break into these money systems and steal whatever they can. They've been successful in stealing millions in "crypto" or digital currencies that will never exist in paper or gold.[181]

It's certainly not far-fetched that machine intelligence will continue to go beyond money transfers and trading and enter the realm of managing these global money systems. Maybe the Federal Reserve, Bank of China, Bank of England, and European Central Bank will form a digital consortium to manage global money supplies and lending. It is entirely possible that such a collaboration could ease the widespread pain of market collapses and recessions—or prevent them altogether. One could argue, given the punishing societal impact of recessions and depressions, that employing machines to spot potential problems and fix them is a reasonable goal.

Yet let's get back to Asimov's rules and play a little logic game. People are behind algorithms and embed human flaws within programs. While we might be able to direct computers to screen out the worst of our tendencies, no program will be entirely free of our flaws. Our greed and fear may even be amplified on a global scale. Panics might be even more severe if our worst instincts are part of the global economic control mechanism. And then there's the premise of the "bad robot" narrative: if robots start thinking—and acting—like people, they *will* break rules, even ones we set for them. That means if we adopt benign neglect without any oversight, then the singularity will look more like Hollywood and less like Valhalla. That means we need to do more work on the ethical and policy side. Governments need to come up with some collaborative guidelines and enforcement on robotic systems.

"AI will reconfigure how society and the economy operate," write Darrell West and John Allen for the Brookings Institution, "and there needs to be 'big picture thinking' on what this will mean for ethics, governance and societal impact. People will need the ability to think broadly about many questions and integrate knowledge from a number of different areas."[182]

In other words, whoever is policing or supervising global AI applications should be a functional Quad I. They should be able to integrate their insights into policies that will protect us from massive unemployment or economic catastrophes. And they should have a strong moral and ethical grounding that respects the brightest and darkest aspects of humanity.

We also need more thinkers like Isaac Asimov, who straddled the worlds of hard science, academia, and popular entertainment. Growing up, I admired him for his writing, but now I appreciate how much of a Quad I he was. Like a lot of kids interested in science, I certainly idolized Albert Einstein, although his genius seemed much too supernatural for me. I couldn't relate to him, even though he played the violin (so do I). Like a barnacle, I really latched onto Asimov, who wrote or edited some 500 books. Although he was a seminal science fiction writer, he also wrote hundreds of nonfiction books on everything from the bible to physics. He was a polymath on steroids. I couldn't wait to check out his latest book. I remember getting the basics on biology, chemistry, physics, and a hundred other subjects from him.

Our first town library was as tiny as a house of knowledge could be: it was a two-story storefront. My most exciting time was when my mother took me there. Over the years, the library moved to progressively larger spaces. Now my hometown of Matteson, Illinois, has a fairly substantial main library.

As a bookish kid. I learned the universe was ever expanding. My curiosity, though, was fueled by technology, although really rudimentary stuff. I played with walkie-talkies and built my own radios. I even had a crude robot. Even as I relished each episode of *Flash Gordon* with its cheesy special effects, I couldn't wait for the next episode. Then Americans stepped on the moon. A new chapter of humanity opened up. It's hard to believe, but a roomful of computers with tape drives powered those missions. Most laptops can process information faster than the "iron" managing the Apollo missions. Asimov was the sparkling narrator of this world. The universe opened up like the massive door of a bank vault.

As I reflect on my childhood, I remember being powered by pure curiosity. While I yearned to be a scientist, there was so much more in the world that I treasured that went beyond measuring the rhythms of the cosmos. I once had a toolbox that I kept my favorite tools in. My dad had given it to me as a portmanteau for my aspirations. On the lid of the steel box I wrote "John F. Wasik, biophysicist." I wanted to know how the universe connected with us organic life forms. How did the solar wind change our moods? Did it cause wars? Did it create life at some point?

There were so many questions then that are *still* vexing us. Will machines give us the answers? I doubt it. But we should be coming up with some rules of engagement over use of information and AI. Einstein and Asimov discovered some important truths. We have much more work to do. To find out where we're going, though, we need to know who we are.

Notes

INTRODUCTION

1. https://obamawhitehouse.archives.gov/sites/whitehouse.gov/files/documents/Artificial-Intelligence-Automation-Economy.PDF p. 2.

2. Ibid.

3. James Manyika, Michael Chui, Mehdi Miremadi, Jacques Bughin, Katy George, Paul Willmott, and Martin Dewhurst, "Harnessing Automation for a Future That Works," McKinsey Global Institute, January, 2017. https://www.mckinsey.com/featured-insights/digital-disruption/harnessing-automation-for-a-future-that-works

4. Ibid.

5. Ibid.

6. Carl Frey and Michael Osborne, "The Future of Employment: How Susceptible Are Jobs to Computerisation?" Oxford Martin School of Business, Sept. 17, 2013. https://www.oxfordmartin.ox.ac.uk/downloads/academic/The_Future_of_Employment.pdf

7. Ibid.

8. Daron Acemoglu and Pascual Restrepo, "Automation and New Tasks: How Automation Displaces and Reinstates Labor," National Bureau of Economic Research/MIT, March 5, 2019. https://economics.mit.edu/files/17023

9. Steve LeVine. "The Problem with Automation," Axios, April 10, 2019. https://www.axios.com/automation-robots-why-theyre-killing-jobs-8de8d871-ef21-43de-99d4-6f4fc60b3020.html

CHAPTER 1

10. Tesla's work and inventions in this section are extensively detailed in my book *Lightning Strikes: Timeless Lessons in Creativity from the Life and Work of Nikola Tesla* (Sterling, 2016).

11. New America Foundation, "World of Drones." https://www .newamerica.org/in-depth/world-of-drones/

12. Miomir Vukobratovic, "Nikola Tesla and Robotics," *Serbian Journal of Electrical Engineering*, November, 2006, pp. 163–175.

13. Ibid., p. 165.

14. John Maynard Keynes, *Economic Possibilities for Our Grandchildren*, from *Essays in Persuasion* (Norton, 1963).

15. I profile Keynes and ideas in greater depth in my book *Keynes's Way to Wealth: Timeless Lesson from the Great Economist* (McGraw-Hill, 2014).

16. Chris Bryant and Elaine He, "The Robot Rampage," Bloomberg View, Jan. 8, 2017. https://www.bloomberg.com/opinion/articles/2017-01-09 /the-robot-threat-donald-trump-isn-t-talking-abou

17. Jeff Guo, "Why We're So Unprepared for the Robot Apocalypse," *The Washington Post*, March 30, 2017. https://www.washingtonpost.com /news/wonk/wp/2017/03/30/were-so-unprepared-for-the-robot-apocalypse /?utm_term=.e12dbeea84b2

18. David Pogue, "The Disruption of Workers by Robots Is About to Take a Giant Leap Forward," Yahoo Finance, April 5, 2017. https://finance.yahoo.com /news/disruption-workers-robots-take-giant-leap-forward-173952383.html

19. Michael Gibbs, "Machines and the Modern-Day Labor Market," *Science Daily*, March 28, 2017.

CHAPTER 2

20. Terry Brown, "The Closing of Wisconsin Steel," *Chicago Tribune*, January 3, 2008. https://www.chicagotribune.com/news/nationworld/politics /chi-chicagodays-wisconsinsteel-story-story.html

I conducted several interviews during December, 2017 and 2018. My reporting for *The Daily Calumet* is in the archives of the Chicago History Museum. Most of my background on the job losses in the steel industry is from my reporting and subsequent research.

21. Joyce Russell, "Industry Defines Northwest Indiana, Then and Now," *Northwest Indiana Times*, March 12, 2017. https://www.nwitimes.com /business/jobs-and-employment/workplace/progress/industry-defines

-northwest-indiana-then-and-now/article_21266072-2b50-5f7f-b98b
-0fd4b4d15991.html

22. Louis Jacobson, "Has Automation Driven Job Losses in the Steel Industry," Politifact, March 8, 2018. https://www.politifact.com/punditfact /statements/2018/mar/08/noah-smith/has-automation-driven-job-losses -steel-industry

23. Elizabeth Svoboda, "Life and Death after the Steel Mills," sapiens .org, Oct. 18, 2017. https://www.sapiens.org/culture/postindustrial-world -chicago-steel

24. "The Future of Jobs Report 2018," World Economic Forum, January, 2018. https://www.weforum.org/reports/the-future-of-jobs-report-2018

25. Ibid.

26. Elizabeth Grieco, "Newsroom Employment Dropped by Nearly a Quarter in Less Than 10 Years, with the Greatest Decline in Newspapers," Pew Research Center, July 30, 2018. http://www.pewresearch.org/fact-tank /2018/07/30/newsroom-employment-dropped-nearly-a-quarter-in-less -than-10-years-with-greatest-decline-at-newspapers

27. U.S. Bureau of Labor Statistics, U.S. Dept. of Labor, "Current Employment Statistics Survey," *Monthly Labor Review*, August, 2016. https://www.bls.gov/opub/mlr/2016/article/current-employment-statistics -survey-100-years-of-employment-hours-and-earnings.htm

28. Robotics Industry Association, "North American Robot Sales Break Record to Start 2018," May 16, 2018. https://www.controleng.com/articles /north-american-robot-sales-break-record-to-start-2018/

29. Michael J. Hicks, "The Myth and Reality of Manufacturing in America," Conexus Indiana (Ball State University), April, 2017. https://conexus .cberdata.org/files/MfgReality.pdf

30. Ibid.

31. Joel Less, "Self-Driving Cars Endanger Millions of American Jobs (and that's okay)," makeuseof.com, June 19, 2015. https://www.makeuseof .com/tag/self-driving-cars-endanger-millions-american-jobs-thats-okay/

32. Ibid.

33. Nanette Byrnes, "As Goldman embraces automation, even the masters of the universe are threatened," MIT Technology Review, Feb. 7, 2017 https://www.technologyreview.com/s/603431/as-goldman-embraces -automation-even-the-masters-of-the-universe-are-threatened/

34. Shelly Palmer, "What will you do after white-collar work," shellyp-almer.com, Aug. 1, 2015. https://www.shellypalmer.com/2015/08/what-will -you-do-after-white-collar-work/

CHAPTER 3

35. Interview with Travis Briggs, Sept 7, 2017 in Chicago.

36. RoboGlobal, 2019 Outlook, www.roboglobal.com

37. Ibid.

38. https://www.cnn.com/2019/04/09/business/walmart-robots-retail
-jobs/index.html

39. Daron Acemoglu and Pascual Restrepo, "Robots and Jobs in the U.S. Labor Market," *NBER Digest*, May, 2017.

40. Ibid.

41. Michael Hicks and Srikant Devaraj, "The Myth and Reality of Manufacturing in America," Conexus Indiana/Ball State University Center for Business and Economic Research, June 2015.

42. Ibid.

43. Anastassia Lauterbach and Andrea Bonime-Blanc, *The Artificial Intelligence Imperative: A Practical Roadmap for Business* (Praeger, 2018), p. 41.

44. "The Future of Jobs Report 2018," The World Economic Forum, p. 9. http://www3.weforum.org/docs/WEF_Future_of_Jobs_2018.pdf

45. Ibid.

46. Frey and Osborne, pp. 70–72.

CHAPTER 4

47. Steve LeVine, "Report: Reskilling Workers Due to Automation Will Cost $34 Billion," Axios, January 23, 2019. https://www.axios.com/davos
-report-reskilling-workers-automation-34-billion-cde16f45-1d15-4018
-82ad-6ad80b3279cc.html

48. Cat Zakrzewski, "Workers in Heartland States Most at Risk of Losing Jobs to AI, New Study Finds," *The Washington Post*, January 24, 2019. https://www.washingtonpost.com/news/powerpost/paloma/the-technology
-202/2019/01/24/the-technology-202-workers-in-heartland-states-most-at
-risk-of-losing-jobs-to-ai-new-study-finds/5c48b28d1b326b29c3778c90
/?utm_term=.f88f76e0828b

49. Martin Ford, *Rise of the Robots: Technology and the Threat of a Jobless Future* (Basic Books, 2015), p. 127.

50. Kevin Roose, "The Hidden Automation Agenda of the Davos Elite," *The New York Times*, January 25, 2019. https://www.nytimes.com/2019/01
/25/technology/automation-davos-world-economic-forum.html

51. Ibid.

52. "Future of Jobs," WEF, p 47.

53. Oxford Study, pp. 57–59.

CHAPTER 5

54. Chicago Innovation Awards, Harris Theater, Chicago, Illinois, Oct. 30. 2018. (I attended). https://www.chicagobusiness.com/john-pletz -technology/chicago-innovation-awards-spotlight-internet-things-and-ai

55. Abbot Labs, Freestyle Libre, https://www.freestylelibre.us

56. Farmer's Fridge, https://www.farmersfridge.com/ourstory

57. Esquify, http://www.esquify.com/

58. https://www.ilholocaustmuseum.org/tas/

59. John Wasik, "Help for a Business Idea Trying to Catch Fire," *The New York Times*, Oct. 12, 2016. https://www.nytimes.com/2016/10/13 /business/smallbusiness/help-for-a-business-idea-trying-to-catch-fire.html

60. https://www.simplemills.com/pages/mission

61. Ibid.

62. https://www.personalcapital.com

63. State Street, "Finance Reimagined: Finding Value in a Digital Age," April, 2017. http://www.statestreet.com/ideas/articles/finance-reimagined -byline.html

64. Ruchir Sharma, "Robots Won't Kill the Global Workforce. They'll Save the Global Economy." *The Washington Post*, Dec. 2, 2016. https://www .washingtonpost.com/posteverything/wp/2016/12/02/robots-wont-kill-the -workforce-theyll-save-the-global-economy/?utm_term=.d5180f7dbf7e

65. Ibid.

66. Steve Lohr, "Robots Will Take Jobs, but not as Fast as Some Fear," *The New York Times*, Jan. 12, 2017. https://www.nytimes.com/2017/01/12 /technology/robots-will-take-jobs-but-not-as-fast-as-some-fear-new-report -says.html

67. Tim Dunlop, "The Robot Debate Is Over: The Jobs Are Gone and They Aren't Coming Back," *The Guardian*, March 30, 2017. https://www .theguardian.com/sustainable-business/2017/mar/31/the-robot-debate-is -over-the-jobs-are-gone-and-they-arent-coming-back

CHAPTER 6

68. Rob Twardock, Dec. 21, 2018 interview, College of Lake County Baxter Innovation Lab, http://home.clcillinois.edu/eng491/personal

69. Ibid.

70. http://www.clcillinois.edu/programs/arm

71. US Fab Lab Network Mission statement, http://usfln.org/about-us /mission/

72. Ibid.

73. https://makerfaire.com/maker-movement

74. https://help.makermedia.com/hc/en-us/articles/204141949-How-many -Maker-Faires-are-there-

75. Chris Matthews, "Bill Gates Says We're on the Verge of These 3 Amazing Technological Advances," *Fortune*, July 27, 2016. https://www .cambridge.org/core/journals/mrs-bulletin/news/bill-gates-says-we-re-on -the-verge-of-these-3-amazing-technological-advances

CHAPTER 7

76. https://oi.uchicago.edu/museum-exhibits/special-exhibits/raiders-lost -journal-hunt-real-indiana-jones

77. Robert Shiller, "Economics and the Human Instincts for Storytell- ing," Neubauer Collegium for Culture and Society Director's Lecture, Jan- uary 26, 2017, University of Chicago Oriental Institute, Chicago.

78. Ibid.

79. Ibid.

80. Alex Garland, director, *Ex Machina*. https://www.imdb.com/title /tt0470752/

81. Katja Grace, John Salvatier, Allan Dafoe, Baobao Zhang, and Owain Evans, "When Will AI Exceed Human Performance, Evidence from AI Experts," *Journal of Artificial Intelligence Research*, May 2018. https://arxiv .org/abs/1705.08807

82. Ibid.

83. Ibid.

84. Jaclyn Peiser, "The Rise of the Robot Reporter," *The New York Times*, Feb. 5, 2019. https://www.nytimes.com/2019/02/05/business/media/artificial -intelligence-journalism-robots.html

85. Ibid.

86. https://en.wikipedia.org/wiki/Chesley_Sullenberger

87. Frey and Osborne, p. 31.

88. Ibid.

89. James Manyika and Kevin Sneader, "AI, Automation and the Future of Work," Rotman Management, Winter 2019, p 41. (Based on their

McKinsey report: https://www.mckinsey.com/featured-insights/future-of-work/ai-automation-and-the-future-of-work-ten-things-to-solve-for)

90. Ibid.

91. Matthew Hutson, "Computers Are Starting to Reason Like Humans," *Science News*, AAAS, June 14, 2017. https://www.sciencemag.org/news/2017/06/computers-are-starting-reason-humans?r3f_986=https://www.google.com

92. Ed Hess, "In the AI Age, 'Being Smart' Will Mean Something Completely Different," *Harvard Business Review*, June 19, 2017. https://hbr.org/2017/06/in-the-ai-age-being-smart-will-mean-something-completely-different

93. Robert Shiller, *Irrational Exuberance* (Princeton University Press, 2005), p. 10.

94. Ibid.

95. Ibid.

CHAPTER 8

96. University of Chicago Gleacher Center, "Bridging the Gap: The Power of Liberal Arts in the Age of the Machine," a presentation and moderated panel, May 31, 2017, Chicago, IL. https://grahamschool.uchicago.edu/news/how-liberal-arts-thrive-business-world

97. Ibid.

98. Ibid.

99. Andrew McAfee and Erik Brynjolfsson, *The Machine Platform Crowd: Harnessing Our Digital Future* (Norton, 2017), p. 333.

100. Martin Seligman, *Homo Prospectus* (Oxford University Press, 2016).

101. Ibid.

102. Ibid.

103. Ibid.

104. Ibid.

105. Ibid.

106. Ibid.

107. Danielle Paquette, "Farmworker vs. Robot," *The Washington Post*, Feb. 17, 2019. https://www.washingtonpost.com/news/national/wp/2019/02/17/feature/inside-the-race-to-replace-farmworkers-with-robots/?utm_term=.11e74f565f00&wpisrc=nl_most&wpmm=1

108. Ibid.

109. Seligman, p. 334.

110. Merriam Webster online, https://www.merriam-webster.com/dictionary/liberal%20arts

111. "What Is Liberal Arts Education?" https://www.topuniversities.com/blog/what-liberal-arts-education

112. Christian Madsbjerg, *Sensemaking: The Power of Humanities in the Age of Algorithm* (Hachette, 2017), p. 6.

113. Ibid.

114. Harriet Zuckerman, "Nobel Laureates in Science: Patterns of Productivity, Collaboration and Authorship," *American Sociological Review*, June, 1967, pp. 391–403. https://www.jstor.org/stable/pdf/2091086.pdf?seq=1/subjects

115. T. L. Andrews, "Robots Won't Take Your Job—They'll Help Make Room for Meaningful Work," Quartz, March 15, 2017. https://qz.com/932417/robots-wont-take-your-job-theyll-help-make-room-for-meaningful-work-instead

116. Ibid.

117. John Allen, "Why We Need to Rethink Education in the Artificial Intelligence Age," Jan. 31, 2019. https://www.brookings.edu/research/why-we-need-to-rethink-education-in-the-artificial-intelligence-age

118. Ibid.

119. Ibid.

CHAPTER 9

The introduction to this chapter is from a meeting in Fox Lake, Illinois, on Feb. 19, 2019.

120. Brad Plumer and Blacki Miglozzi, "How to Cut U.S. Emissions Faster? Do What These Countries Are Doing," *The New York Times*, Feb. 13, 2019. https://www.nytimes.com/interactive/2019/02/13/climate/cut-us-emissions-with-policies-from-other-countries.html

121. Ibid.

122. The National Science Foundation, "Convergence Research at NSF," https://www.nsf.gov/od/oia/convergence/index.jsp

123. Cathy Davidson, *The New Education* (Basic Books, 2017). https://www.amazon.com/gp/product/0465079725/ref=dbs_a_def_rwt_bibl_vppi_i0

124. Cathy Davidson, "Education for the Gig Economy," Chicago Humanities Festival lecture, Nov. 7, 2017, Chicago, Illinois. https://www.chicagohumanities.org/media/cathy-davidson-education-gig-economy

125. Ibid.

126. Adam Satariano, Elian Peltier, and Dmitry Kostyukov, "Meet Zora, the Robot Caregiver," *The New York Times*, Nov. 23, 2018.

127. Ibid.

128. Ibid.

129. Patrick Cook-Deegan and Bob Lenz, "Rebooting the American High School with Neuroscience and Purpose Learning," Stanford Social Innovation Review webinar, May 24, 2017.

130. Ibid.

131. Ibid.

132. https://www.pltw.org/about-us/our-approach

133. Beau Lotto, *Deviate: The Science of Seeing Differently* (Hachette, 2017), p. 280. https://www.amazon.com/Deviate-Science-Differently-Beau-Lotto-ebook/dp/B01922I10M/ref=tmm_kin_swatch_0?_encoding=UTF8&qid=&sr=

134. Oren Cass, "College Isn't for Everyone," *The New York Times*, Dec. 12, 2018.

135. https://studentloanhero.com/student-loan-debt-statistics

136. Adam Grant, "What Straight-A Students Get Wrong," *The New York Times*, Dec. 9, 2018.

137. Karen Christiansen, "Questions for Michael Platt," *Rotman* magazine, Jan. 1, 2019. P. 119.

CHAPTER 10

138. David Pogue, "The Disruption of Workers by Robots Is About to Take a Giant Leap Forward," Yahoo Finance, April 5, 2017. https://finance.yahoo.com/news/disruption-workers-robots-take-giant-leap-forward-173952383.html

139. Edward Hess and Katherine Ludwig, *Humility is the New Smart: Rethinking Human Excellence in the Smart Machine Age* (Berrett-Koehler, 2017), p. 5.

140. Ibid.

141. Ibid.

142. Darrell West and John Allen, "How Artificial Intelligence Is Transforming the World," Brookings Institution Report, April 24, 2018. https://www.brookings.edu/research/how-artificial-intelligence-is-transforming-the-world/

143. Lauterbach and Bonime-Blanc, p. 209.

144. Jeremy Rifkin, *The Third Industrial Revolution: How Lateral Power Is Transforming Energy, The Economy and the World* (Palgrave Macmillan, 2011), p. 265.

145. McAfee and Erik Brynjolfsson, p. 257.

146. Tony Wagner and Ted Dintersmith, *Most Likely to Succeed: Preparing Our Kids for the Innovation Era* (Scribner, 2015), p. 248.

147. Ibid.

148. Genevieve Shanahan, "France: Piketty's Comments on Basic Income Cause Confusion," BIEN, Feb. 3, 2017. https://basicincome.org/news/2017 /02/france-pikettys-basic-income-comments-cause-confusion/

149. Max Tegmark, *Life 3.0: Being Human in the Age of Artificial Intelligence* (Knopf, 2017), p. 128

150. Ibid.

151. Ibid.

AFTERWORD

152. Elizabeth Dwoskin, "Stanford Helped Pioneer Artificial Intelligence. Now It Wants to Put Humans at the Center," *The Washington Post*, March 18, 2019. https://www.washingtonpost.com/technology/2019/03/18 /stanford-helped-pioneer-artificial-intelligence-now-university-wants-put -humans-its-center/?utm_term=.38c9d5203065

APPENDIX

153. U.S. Bureau of Labor Statistics, "Occupational Outlook Handbook," https://www.bls.gov/ooh/fastest-growing.htm

154. Jason Schenker, "How to Survive the Robocalypse," Bloomberg News, March 6, 2017. https://www.bloomberg.com/opinion/articles/2017-03 -06/how-to-survive-the-robocalypse

155. Shelly Palmer, "The 5 Jobs Robots Will Take Last," Linked-In Pulse, March 5, 2017. https://www.shellypalmer.com/2017/03/5-jobs-robots -will-take-last

156. Nick Polson and James Scott, *AIQ: How People and Machines Are Smarter Together* (St. Martin's Press, 2018), p. 227.

157. Mihaly Csikszentmihalyi, *Flow: The Psychology of Optimal Experience* (Harper & Row, 1990), p. 40.

158. UNESCO Creative Cities Network, https://en.unesco.org/news/64
-cities-join-unesco-creative-cities-network

159. Richard Florida, "How Culture Shapes Economic Development,"
citylab, June 7, 2018. https://www.citylab.com/life/2018/06/how-culture
-shapes-economic-development/562328

160. Joe Davis, "Global Economic Potential," FPA Chicago, Oct. 4, 2018
(keynote address), Hyatt Chicago Hotel. https://www.investordaily.com.au
/markets/44420-trade-in-innovation-can-predict-future-growth

161. Ibid.

162. NerdWallet Compound Interest Calculator, https://www.nerdwallet
.com/banking/calculator/compound-interest-calculator

163. Tim Harford, *Fifty Inventions That Shaped the Modern Economy*
(Riverhead, 2017), p. 11.

164. Wendell Berry, *Sex, Economy, Freedom and Community* (Pantheon,
1992), p. 25.

165. Susan Bauer, *Quiet: The Power of Introverts in a World That Can't
Stop Talking* (Broadway Books, 2012), p. 11.

166. Susan Wise Bauer, *The Well-Educated Mind: A Guide to the Classical Education You Never Had* (Norton, 2003), p. 39.

167. Viktor Frankl, *Man's Search for Meaning* (Simon & Schuster, 1984),
p. 141.

168. Daniel Goleman, *Focus: The Hidden Driver of Excellence* (Harper,
2013), p. 16.

169. Ibid.

170. Daniel Goleman, Paul Kaufman and Michael Ray, *The Creative
Spirit* (Dutton, 1992), p. 65.

171. Joel Levey and Michelle Levey, *Living in Balance: A Dynamic
Approach for Creating Harmony and Wholeness in a Chaotic World*
(Conari Press, 1998), p. 286.

172. Ibid.

173. Marilyn Schlitz, Cassandra Vieten, and Tina Amorok, *Living
Deeply: The Art & Science of Transformation in Everyday Life* (New Har-
binger, 2007).

POSTSCRIPT

174. Dom Galeon and Christianna Reedy, "Ray Kurzweil Claims Singularity Will Happen by 2045," *Futurism*, March 14, 2017.

175. https://www.turing.org.uk

176. Ibid.

177. Ibid.

178. Ibid.

179. Isaac Asimov, *I, Robot* (Doubleday, 1940–1950).

180. Ibid.

181. I've written about cryptocurrencies extensively for my *Forbes* blog *Bamboozlement*.

182. Ibid.

Essential Reading

Mihaly Csikszentmihalyi, *Flow: The Psychology of Optimal Experience* (Harper & Row, 1990).

Cathy Davidson, *The New Education* (Basic Books, 2017).

Martin Ford, *Rise of the Robots* (Basic Books, 2015).

Edward Hess and Katherine Ludwig, *Humility Is the New Smart: Rethinking Human Excellence in the Smart Machine Age* (Berrett-Koehler, 2017).

Anastassia Lauterbach and Andrea Bonime-Blanc, *The Artificial Intelligence Imperative: A Practical Roadmap for Business* (Praeger, 2018).

Beau Lotto, *Deviate: The Science of Seeing Differently* (Hachette, 2017).

Christian Madsbjerg, *Sensemaking: The Power of Humanities in the Age of Algorithm* (Hachette, 2017).

Andrew McAfee and Erik Brynjolfsson, *The Machine Platform Crowd: Harnessing Our Digital Future* (Norton, 2017).

Nick Polson and James Scott, *AIQ: How People and Machines Are Smarter Together* (St. Martin's Press, 2018).

Jeremy Rifkin, *The Third Industrial Revolution: How Lateral Power is Transforming Energy, The Economy and the World* (Palgrave Macmillan, 2011).

Martin Seligman, *Homo Prospectus* (Oxford University Press, 2016).

Robert Shiller, *Irrational Exuberance* (Princeton, 2005), 2nd edition.

Michael Taylor, *The Financial Rules for New College Graduates* (Praeger, 2018).

Max Tegmark, *Life 3.0: Being Human in the Age of Artificial Intelligence* (Knopf, 2017).

Tony Wagner and Ted Dintersmith, *Most Likely to Succeed: Preparing Our Kids for the Innovation Era* (Scribner, 2015).

John F. Wasik, *Keynes's Way to Wealth: Timeless Lessons from the Great Economist* (McGraw-Hill, 2014).

John F. Wasik, *Lightning Strikes: Timeless Lessons in Creativity from the Life and Work of Nikola Tesla* (Sterling, 2016).

Index

About the Author

John F. Wasik is the author of 18 books, including *Lightning Strikes: Timeless Lessons in Creativity from the Life and Work of Nikola Tesla* (2016). A professional speaker and journalist, he has entertained audiences across North America. As a journalist, he's contributed to *The New York Times, Wall Street Journal*, Bloomberg News, Forbes and Reuters. His articles have appeared in newspapers on five continents. A commissioner for Lake County, Illinois, he resides in Grayslake, Illinois, with his wife and two daughters. He received his B.A. and M.A. from the University of Illinois at Chicago.